A Sickle Crisis?

A report of the National Confidential Enquiry
into Patient Outcome and Death (2008)

Compiled by:

S B Lucas FRCP FRCPath
Clinical Co-ordinator

D G Mason FFARCS
Clinical Co-ordinator

M Mason PhD
Chief Executive

D Weyman BSc (Hons)
Researcher

On behalf of NCEPOD

M Jarmulowicz FRCPath
D Justins MB, BS, FRCA
S Lawson BSC, MBChB, MRCP, FRCPath
L Oni OBE B ED (Hons), LHV, NT, RM
N Parker FRCP FRCPath
A Streetly BA, MB BChir, MSC, FFPH

Contents

Acknowledgements

This report, published by NCEPOD, could not have been achieved without the support of a wide range of individuals and organisations.

Our particular thanks go to:

The Expert Group who advised NCEPOD:

Dr Stephen Bridgman
Associate Director of Public Health
Countess of Chester Health Park

Dr Phil Darbyshire
Paediatric Haematologist
Birmingham Childrenís Hospital

Ms Catherine Dhanda
Clinical Lead Nurse for Haemoglobinopathies
Sickle Cell and Thalasssaemia Centre
Sandwell and West Birmingham NHS Trust

Dr Jane Logan
General Practitioner
Mawbey Brough Health Centre

Dr Asa'ah Nkohkwo
Director
Sickle Cell Society

Dr Colin Sandiford
Patient representative

Dr Allison Streetly
Programme Director
NHS Sickle Cell & Thalassaemia Screening Programme

Dr Josh Wright
Haematologist
Sheffield Teaching Hospitals NHS Foundation Trust

The Advisors who reviewed the cases:

Dr Michael Jarmulowicz
Associate Medical Director
Bostwick Laboratories

Dr Doug Justins
Pain specialist/NCEPOD Trustee
Guyís and St Thomasí NHS Trust

Dr Sarah Lawson
Paediatric Haematologist
Birmingham Childrenís Hospital

Dr Lola Oni
Professional Services Director/ Specialist Nurse
Brent Sickle Cell and Thalassaemia Centre

Dr Norman Parker
Haematologist
Whittington Hospital NHS Trust

The organisations that provided funding to cover the cost of this study:

Aspen Healthcare
Benenden Hospital
BMI Healthcare
BUPA
Capio Group
Covenant Healthcare
Cromwell Hospital
Department of Health, Social Services and Public Safety (Northern Ireland)
Fairfield Independent Hospital
HCA International
Horder Centre
Hospital Management Trust

ACKNOWLEDGEMENTS

Hospital of St John and St Elizabeth
Isle of Man Health and Social Security Department
King Edward VII Hospital
King Edward VIIs Hospital Sister Agnes
London Clinic
McIndoe Surgical Centre
Mount Alvernia Hospital
National Patient Safety Agency
Netcare Healthcare
New Victoria Hospital
North Wales Medical Centre
Nuffield Hospitals
Spencer Wing, Queen Elizabeth the Queen Mother Hospital
St Anthonyís Hospital
St Josephís Hospital
States of Guernsey, Health and Social Services
States of Jersey, Health and Social Services
Ulster Independent Clinic

Institute of Healthcare Management
Royal College of Anaesthetists
Royal College of Child Health and Paediatrics
Royal College of General Practitioners
Royal College of Nursing
Royal College of Obstetricians and Gynaecologists
Royal College of Ophthalmologists
Royal College of Pathologists
Royal College of Physicians of London
Royal College of Radiologists
Royal College of Surgeons of England

The authors and Trustees of NCEPOD would particularly like to thank the NCEPOD staff for their hard work in collecting and analysing the data for this study:

Robert Alleway, Sabah Begg, Maurice Blackman, Heather Cooper, Clare Holtby, Kathryn Kelly, Dolores Jarman, Rakhee Lakhani, Karen Protopapa and Neil Smith.

The professional organisations that support our work and who constitute our Steering Group:

Association of Anaesthetists of Great Britain and Ireland
Association of Surgeons of Great Britain and Ireland
College of Emergency Medicine
Coronersí Society of England and Wales
Faculty of Dental Surgery of the Royal College of Surgeons of England
Faculty of Public Health of the Royal College of Physicians of the UK

DISCLAIMER

This work was undertaken by NCEPOD, which received funding for this report from the National Patient Safety Agency. The views expressed in this publication are those of the authors and not necessarily those of the Agency.

4

Foreword

For the National Confidential Enquiry into Patient Outcome and Death this report on sickle cell disease and thalassaemia is one of a new wave of studies. NCEPOD started life investigating the circumstances of perioperative death but broadened its remit to look at the care of non-surgical patients and to address outcomes other than death. Previous studies have usually been defined by a particular clinical setting and a process of care such as out-of-hours surgery, emergency admissions or care of the severely injured, and it was this setting which defined the patient group. In the study we focus on a group of patients who have a specific diagnosis which is with them throughout life. For these patients there is a lifetime of episodic illness.

The haemoglobinopathies are the most prevalent inherited diseases of mankind, constituting a major health problem in many countries. At the level of the beta globin chain in the all-important haemoglobin molecule, the impact of the single point mutation (in sickle patients) or abnormal developmental switching (in beta thalassaemia) is huge. Until recently, life expectancy was short. But greater scientific understanding, better drug therapy, and the implementation of more standardised protocols mean that people with sickle and thalassaemia survive well into adult life.

The demography is shifting, particularly for sickle cell disease. Because of immigration from Africa and the Caribbean, there are more sickle cell adults and children arriving in the United Kingdom, and more mothers delivering affected babies. England now has complete neonatal screening for haemoglobinopathy; Wales and Scotland are rolling it out, and we discover that the frequency of the disease is now at least as common as the more familiar cystic fibrosis. Whilst an increasing proportion of affected people will be known from birth, the undiagnosed will continue to present, ill, at health centres. And from being mainly the preserve of London and the West Midlands, sickle patients increasingly present anywhere in the UK.

Managing the haemoglobinopathies is a complex multi-disciplinary process because of the key role of haemoglobin and red blood cells in all bodily functions. It has been apparent for some time that the quality of medical experience around haemoglobinopathy is patchy and not universal. This applies to initial diagnosis, crisis management, pain relief and the many other complications that are referred to in this report.

So for all these reasons, NCEPOD was pleased to undertake a review of current haemoglobinopathy mortality, to obtain broad baseline data and make recommendations to alter practice. In this way, we hope to contribute to improving the quality of life of patients – whose numbers and attendances at health care centres are inevitably going to increase.

Sebastian Lucas
NCEPOD Clinical Co-ordinator

Tom Treasure
NCEPOD Chairman

Principal Recommendations

- In our multi-racial society, it is essential that all doctors should have a basic understanding of the implications of thalassaemia and sickle cell trait. (General Medical Council)

- As a minimum, the Department of Health guidance regarding vaccination and prophylactic antibiotics should be followed in order to prevent sepsis from hyposplenism. (Primary Care Trusts)

- A multidisciplinary and multi-agency approach is needed in the ongoing pain management of patients with sickle cell disease – essentially this takes place outside hospitals for the majority of patients. (Primary and Secondary Care Trusts)

- Regular assessment of acute pain, sedation and respiratory rate should be undertaken and recorded for all patients admitted with sickle cell disease. The frequency of these observations should reflect the degree of pain and dose of opioids administered, to allow recognition of opioid overdose. The development of "track & trigger" systems would greatly enhance better pain control and patient safety. (Clinical Directors)

- All staff should be aware that people with sickle cell disease are subject to the diseases that other patients suffer from as well. If there is uncertainty as to whether the problem is sickle cell related, advice should be sought from an experienced clinician. (Clinical Directors)

- All sickle cell disease patients should have a carefully maintained fluid balance chart for the duration of their admission. (Nurses)

- Patients with sickle cell disease or beta thalassaemia major should be managed by, or have access to, clinicians with experience of haemoglobinopathy management. (Primary and Secondary Care Trusts)

- Healthcare centres responsible for the management of patients with haemoglobinopathies should have access to protocols/guidelines from their regional specialist centre. (Primary and Secondary Care Trusts)

- Cause of death in sickle cell disease patients must be better evaluated, whether by clinicians reviewing the records and writing a death certificate or by pathologists performing an autopsy. Clinico-pathological correlation is critical in this complex disease. (Clinicians and Pathologists)

- A national database of patients with haemoglobinopathies should be developed and maintained, to include standardised information on death, for regular audit purposes. (Department of Health)

1 – Introduction

This report reviews the circumstances around deaths in patients with haemoglobinopathies - sickle cell disease and beta thalassaemia – in the 21st century in England, Wales, Northern Ireland and the Offshore Islands. The National Confidential Enquiry into Patient Outcome and Death (NCEPOD) was interested in ascertaining remediable factors in the prophylaxis and management of the clinical syndromes caused by:

- Sickle cell anaemia (HbSS)
- Sickle haemoglobin C (HbSC)
- Sickle haemoglobin D (HbSD)
- Sickle ß-thalassaemia (HbS ß-Thal)
- ß-thalassaemia major
- ß-thalassaemia intermedia.

Epidemiology – global and UK

Haemoglobin disorders (sickle cell disease and alpha & beta thalassaemias) are a global public health issue. They are the world's most common cause of genetic defects, with annual estimates of 300-500,000 births across 193 countries [1, 2]. The World Health Organisation (WHO) estimates that sickle cell disease causes nine percent of deaths in under five year olds in Africa (up to 15% in some countries in West Africa), with infection being the main cause of death [3]. Sickle cell disease and thalassaemia are now WHO priorities, with recent resolutions to support the development of services, given their increasing visibility as health services have developed.

In recent decades in Europe, whilst the overall birth prevalence is lower, there has been a rapid increase in the size of the affected sickle cell disease population, to a lesser degree the thalassaemic population, particularly in urban areas [4].

UK estimates of numbers of affected individuals

National registers do not exist for these conditions. Best estimates suggest that there are approximately 12,000 patients with sickle cell disease and approximately 700-800 thalassaemia patients in the UK [5]. These estimates are based on the assumption that approximately half of patients are admitted in any one year and are useful for service planning purposes, even if not completely accurate. The development of a national haemoglobinopathy register has recently been supported by the Department of Health and it is hoped that in the future more accurate information on the number of affected patients will be available.

Hospital admissions

Across England in 2005-06, admission rates for sickle cell disease increased with age from 13 admissions per 100,000 aged under one year to 38 per 100,000 in the 15-18 age group. The overall admission rate for 0-18 year olds is 28 per 100,000. London has one of the largest cohorts of haemoglobinopathy patients in the UK and is used as an example in this section to illustrate hospital admissions. However, three quarters of all sickle cell disease admissions are for London residents and it is now one of the commonest reasons for admission to hospital and has the highest rate of multiple admissions for individual patients [6, 7]. Within London, distribution of sickle cell disease shows wide variation, with 80% of all admissions living in the two most deprived quintiles of the population (50% in the most deprived quintile) as assessed by post code of residence. This is compared with 60% (30%) for all admissions.

Admissions peak in the 25-34 year old age group and decline sharply after age 45-54 years. Time trends show some recent reductions in admission rates, in some areas, attributed to better community services. Wide variations in admission rates per patient suggest that there is considerable scope for better management of patients. In 2005-06, there were 13,000 episodes for London residents. The number of individuals identified in this London analysis increased from 3,200 in 2000-01 to 4,600 in 2005-06.

Newborn sickle cell disease screening

Newborn sickle cell disease screening implementation across England was completed in July 2006. In Wales, Scotland and Northern Ireland, where the prevalence is lower, but increasing, there are not yet formal newborn screening programmes; although Scotland is in the process of developing one. The screening programme is able to identify a number of abnormalities in haemoglobin; children with homozygous sickle cell disease will be identified as having haemoglobin F, the normal neonatal type of haemoglobin, and S for sickle haemoglobin. This is written as HbF/S. Children who have inherited haemoglobin S and C, another clinically important type, will be described as having HbF/SC. Information from the NHS Sickle Cell and Thalassaemia Screening Programme shows that in 2004-05, with screening results from almost 400,000 babies (373,069), there were 166 HbF/S, 52 HbF/SC and 26 other clinically significant screening results. Provisional figures for 2005-06 show that from almost 500,000 babies there were 217 HbF/S, 71 HbF/SC and 26 other clinically significant results – affecting over 300 births in total [8]. When national figures are available, the birth prevalence of these conditions is likely to be between 1:2000 and 1:2500 for England, making it at least as common as cystic fibrosis at birth. These figures exclude babies who migrate into the UK after birth. Reports from several centres are that an almost equal number of children seen in the clinic are arrivals after birth, but robust numbers are not available and only symptomatic cases will be seen [9].

Pathophysiology of sickle cell disease

Since the events underlying severe morbidity and mortality in sickle cell disease are complex and incompletely understood, it is worth summarising the current understanding of the morbid anatomy of these diseases.

Because of the abnormal beta globin chain, red cell survival is curtailed and there is chronic anaemia. Even more important is polymerisation of haemoglobin S (HbS) within red cells, resulting in the irreversible sickling of red cells under certain physical conditions [10-12]. The consequences are numerous and affect most of the organs in the body:

1. Haemolysis resulting in anaemia.
2. Sickle cell obstruction of small vessels causing ischaemic damage:
   a. in bones this is the origin of the sickle bone pain and the source of fat and marrow embolism; resulting in avascular necrosis and local infection (osteomyelitis);
   b. in lungs it may cause the acute chest syndrome;
   c. in kidneys it causes medullary damage with impaired urinary concentrating ability;
   d. in skin it causes chronic leg ulcers;
   e. cumulatively it can result in multi-organ failure.
3. Sequestration of sickle cells in e.g. spleen and liver, causing sequestration crises.

4. Sickle cell/endothelial cell interaction and cumulative vascular damage in:
   a. lungs, causing pulmonary hypertension;
   b. the brain, causing arterial abnormalities and stroke (ischaemic and haemorrhagic);
   c. kidneys, causing glomerular renal failure;
   d. skin, causing leg ulcers.
5. Progressive ischaemic atrophy of the spleen from ischaemia, increasing the risk of sepsis (particularly pneumococcal).
6. Haemolysis resulting in gall stones and related diseases.

In addition, there are the complications of therapy and prophylaxis for sickle cell disease, namely:
1. Blood transfusion causing iron overload and sensitisation to blood group antigens.
2. Blood-born infections in the transfusions e.g. Hepatitis B & C viruses, and HIV.
3. Opioids and their potential complications including dependency.
4. Hydroxycarbamide (previously termed hydroxyurea) therapy can cause neutropaenia.

Pathophysiology of beta thalassaemia

In thalassaemia, red cell release from the bone marrow is greatly reduced due to inadequate beta globin chain production. The bone marrow expands but is insufficient to maintain haemoglobin level. Life-long red cell transfusions are required. The pathology arises from iron overload and this causes damage to the heart, liver and endocrine organs, such as the pancreas, causing diabetes. These changes are caused by the blood transfusions, which are required to sustain life, with concomitant haemosiderosis. Iron chelation therapy is standard, but iron overload remains a problem where compliance with treatment is poor. Recent developments in the production of oral chelators and the use of combinations [13] may bring further improvements. Exposure to infected blood products, before routine screening was implemented, also exposed this group of patients to complications such as Hepatitis C.

Mortality of sickle cell disease

Whilst data on the causes of major morbidity and mortality in sickle cell disease patients have been published from the USA and the Caribbean (particularly Jamaica, where the UK Medical Research Council has a specialist sickle cell unit [14]) little information has come from Europe and the UK. There is not a UK register of sickle cell disease related deaths and there has never previously been a national survey of these deaths. This is despite the increasing number of sickle cell gene-carrying persons (with increasing numbers of HbSS and HbSC patients) due to immigration and births in the UK.

The largest autopsy series of sickle cell disease (HbSS, HbSC and HbS-beta-thalassaemia patients) (n=306) was from a specialist centre in the USA, covering the years 1929-1996 [15]. The age at death in this series rose progressively after the 1950s, reflecting improved management and survival. Overall, the commonest cause of death at all periods was infection (bacterial and viral agents identified). Stroke accounted for up to 10% of deaths. In this series, only 8% of deaths were not sickle-related.

The two available UK studies are from one centre in London [16] covering 18 deaths over the period 1974-1989, and from four centres in England and France, examining 61 patients over the period 1990-1999 [17].

The earlier study had patients aged from 18 months to 54 years and included autopsy data which identified the following causes of death:

Acute splenic sequestration	2 (both under 5 years of age)
Pneumococcal sepsis	1
Acute chest syndrome	9
Stroke	2
Pulmonary artery thrombosis	1
Asthma	1
Unknown	2

This study emphasised the importance of the acute chest syndrome (ACS) in sickle cell disease.

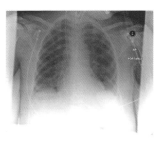 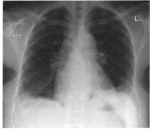

Acute chest syndrome

The European study, from a decade later, studied only adults (n=61, mean age 32 years), and classified deaths into four pathophysiological categories and others[17]:

Acute sickle related vaso-occlusion (mainly ACS, multi-organ failure, and acute stroke)	27
Chronic sickle-related organ failure (debilitating stoke, congestive cardiac failure, chronic renal failure, pulmonary hypertension, cirrhosis)	10
Infection/sepsis (Streptococcus pneumoniae in 4)	10
Unknown (death at home)	8
Others	
Suicide	2
Refusal of care	2
Post-liver biopsy haemorrhage	1
Digitalis intoxication	1

This study included both HbSS and HbSC patients, and pregnant women. It emphasised that adult deaths are multifactorial and noted that one third of patients who died had only apparently mild sickle cell disease before sudden collapse (mainly from acute chest syndrome).

Management of haemoglobinopathies

The management of the inherited haemoglobinopathies has changed radically over the last 30 years, with significant prolongation of life expectancy.

The changing patterns of the clinical pathology and management of sickle cell disease are reflected by the following:

1. Until about the last 30 years, childhood mortality was very high and survival into adulthood uncommon [18, 19].
2. With improved medical care, survival into adulthood is now common [20] and most sickle-related deaths are in adults in economically developed countries.
3. Medical care has shifted from in-patient to out-patient care, reflecting the changes in treatment and prophylaxis.

Antenatal screening and diagnosis is available for those at risk of sickle cell disorders, but the uptake of this service is lower than for those affected by thalassaemia. NHS hospitals that see significant numbers of patients with sickle cell disease have developed local protocols for their management, including: antibiotic prophylaxis, hydroxycarbamide treatment and pneumococcal vaccination. There are national guidelines for managing acute sickle-related pain [21] and recommendations for transcranial Doppler ultrasound to detect stroke risk in children [22]. Furthermore, there are overarching guidelines available for clinical care for children with sickle cell disease [23].

In thalassaemia, the major effort has gone into prevention through screening and genetic counselling and, if requested, early termination of thalassaemia major foetuses. Management of patients still revolves around red cell transfusions and controlling the complications of iron overload on the heart, liver and other critical organs. With better chelation, there has been a major improvement in life expectancy as demonstrated in international studies [13, 24]. Even with this therapy, many patients suffer significant morbidity in early adult life. There has not been any formal organisation supporting the care of these patients in the UK.

The families of individuals with sickle cell trait, detected by the neonatal screening process, are now offered appropriate counselling regarding future genetic risk.

The Department of Health has recently supported the development of organised clinical networks of care in paediatric haemoglobinopathy which will address some of the issues of access and quality.

Current specific management of sickle cell disease patients

The modern long-term management of patients with sickle cell disease includes the following preventive interventions (derived from UK Guidelines [21, 25, 26]):

Category	Intervention
1. Newborn screening	England - policy at birth.
2. Infection	Prophylactic penicillin. Pneumococcal vaccination.
3. Anaemia	Red cell transfusion. Prevention of iron overload. Prevention of blood borne virus infections by product screening.
4. Acute chest syndrome and chronic lung injury prevention	Red cell transfusion. Prevention with Antibiotic therapy hydroxycarbamide. Monitoring pulmonary function. Screening for pulmonary hypertension.
5. Maintenance of renal function	ACE inhibitors for proteinuria. Renal transplantation.
6. Painful crisis	Hydroxycarbamide therapy Improved regimens for acute pain relief. Patient controlled analgesia.
7. Priapism	Adrenergic agonist. Anti-androgen therapy.
8. Safer surgery	Pre-operative transfusion. Appropriate anaesthesia and post-operative care.

Category	Intervention
9. Gallbladder disease	Laparoscopic cholecystectomy.
10. Avascular necrosis of hip	Decompression coring procedures. Hip replacement surgery.
11. Brain injury (stroke) prevention	Screening with transcranial Doppler ultrasound in children.
12. Chronic leg ulcers	Red cell transfusion.
13. Acute sequestration prevention	Transfusion and Hydroxycarbamide. Splenectomy in some cases.
14. Chronic severe disease	Chronic transfusion and hydroxycarbamide. Bone marrow transplantation.
15. Psycho-social issues	Community care nursing. Specialist psychological care in sickle units. Sickle cell disease day units.
16. General overall care	Appointment of haemoglobinopathy clinical specialists in central units.
17. Pregnancy	Joint care by specialist obstetrician and haematologist.

There are new emerging therapeutic agents and processes for sickle cell disease [25], but none of the patients in this study were known to be receiving them.

Rationale for this study

Haemoglobinopathy care in the UK is changing substantially. There is now a neonatal screening programme in England and national guidelines for clinical care in adults are being developed. Patient care is becoming much more focussed on the prevention of complications and the Department of Health is facilitating the development of regional networks for paediatric haemoglobinopathies.

There have been periodic limited surveys of morbidity and mortality for sickle cell disease and thalassaemia patients in the UK, but no previous national survey and none with casenote review.

The sickle cell disease autopsy

A further reason for NCEPOD to investigate the sickle cell diseases arose from incidental review of the reports and tissue material from autopsies performed upon sickle cell disease patients. These were mostly coronial autopsies, rather than hospital autopsies [16], and review showed that they were poorly performed and often misinterpreted. This reflects a lack of training and knowledge about, and lack of experience in, the evaluation of sickle cell disease pathology among pathologists in the UK. Secondarily, it reflects the limited remit of the coronial autopsy in determining the cause of death in these often complex cases, where an apparently natural 'sickle cell disease' cause of death usually suffices [27].

Thus, NCEPOD believed it was timely to review the mortality related to the haemoglobinopathies in England, Wales, Northern Ireland and the Offshore Islands, to identify specific remediable factors for these particular diseases, over and above the factors identified from previous NCEPOD studies of other complex multi-organ diseases.

References

1. Weatherall D, Akinyanju O, Fucharoen S *et al.* Inherited Disorders of Haemoglobin. *Disease Control Priorities in Developing Countries (2nd Edition)*, 663-680. New York: Oxford University Press. 2006 DO1: 10.1596/978-0-821-36179-5/Chpt-34. *http://www.dcp2.org/pubs/DCP*

2. Christianson A, Howson CP, Modell B. 2006. The March of Dimes Global Report on Birth Defects. The Hidden Toll of Dying and Disabled Children. March of Dimes Birth Defects Foundation. White Plains, New York. [Online] [access 2006 September]. *http://mod.hoggmsnpt.com/MOD-Report.pdf*

3. World Health Organisation. 2006. Sickle-cell anaemia: Report by the secretariat. [Online] [access 2006 October]. *http://www.who.int/gb/ebwha/pdf_files/WHA59/A59_9-en.pdf*

4. Modell B, Darlison M, Birgens H *et al. Epidemiology of haemoglobin disorders in Europe: an overview.* Scand J Clin Lab Invest 2007;67:39-70.

5. Streetly A, Maxwell K, Mejia A. Sickle Cell disorders in Greater London: a needs assessment of screening and care services. Fair Shares for London Report. London: United Medical and Dental Schools Department of Public Health Medicine, 1997.

6. London Health Observatory. 2005. Analysis Of Frequent Users, 2002/03, Local Authority Level. [Online] [access 2006 September]. *http://www.lho.org.uk/viewResource.aspx?id=9736*

7. London Health Observatory. 2006. Analysis of Frequent Hospital Users, by PCT 2003/4. [Online] [access 2006 September]. *http://www.lho.org.uk/viewResource.aspx?id=10286*

8. Streetly A, Clarke M, Downing M *et al. Implementation of the universal newborn screening programme for sickle cell disease in England: results for 2003-2005.* J Med Screening (in press).

9. Personal communication between expert group member and a paediatric haematologist.

10. Stuart MJ, Nagel RL. *Sickle cell disease.* Lancet, 2004:364:1343-60.

11. Serjeant GR, Serjeant BE. Sickle Cell Disease, 3rd edn, Oxford University Press, Oxford, 2001

12. Lucas SB. *The morbid anatomy of sickle cell disease and sickle cell trait* pp 45-62 in *Practical Management of the Haemoglobinopathies.* Okpala I, ed., Blackwell, Oxford, 2004.

13. Telfer P, Coen PG, Christou S *et al. Survival of medically treated thalassaemia patients in Cyprus. Trends and risks factors over the period 1980-2004.* Haematologica 2004:91:1187-92.

14. Thomas AN, Pattison C, Serjeant GR. *Causes of death in sickle cell disease in Jamaica.* BMJ 1982;285:633-7.

15. Manci EA, Culberson DE, Yang YM. *et al, Causes of death in sickle cell disease: an autopsy study*, British Journal of Haematology 2003:123:359-365.

16. Gray A, Anionwu EN, Davies SC, Brozovic M. *Patterns of mortality in sickle cell disease in the United Kingdom*. Journal of Clinical Pathology 1991;44:459-63.

17. Perronne V, Roberts-Harewood M, Bachir D *et al*. *Patterns of mortality in sickle cell disease in adults in France and England*. Haematology Journal 2002;3:56-60

18. Serjeant GR. *Sickle cell disease*. Lancet 1997;350:725-30.

19. Quinn CT, Rogers ZR, Buchanan GR. *Survival of children with sickle cell disease*. Blood 2004;103(11):4023-7.

20. Telfer P, Coen P, Chakravorty S *et al*. *Clinical outcomes in children with sickle cell disease living in England*: a neonatal cohort in East London. Haematologica 2007;92:905-921.

21. Rees DC, Olujohungbe AD, Parker NE *et al*. *Guidelines for the management of the acute painful crisis in sickle cell disease*. British Journal of Haematology 2003;120:744-52.

22. Stroke in childhood: Clinical guidelines for diagnosis, management and rehabilitation. Paediatric Stroke Working Party, Clinical Effectiveness and Evaluation Unit, Royal College of Physicians, 2004.

23. Dick M. Sickle Cell Disease in Childhood, Standards and Guidelines in Clinical Care. For the UK Forum on Haemoglobin Disorders. NHS Sickle Cell and Thalassaemia Screening Programme in partnership with the Sickle Cell Society 2006.

24. Borgna-Pignatti C, Rugolotto S, De Stefano P *et al. Survival and complications in patients with thalassemia major treated with transfusion and deferoxamine*. Haematologica 2004;89(10):1187-93.

25. Vichinsky EP. *New therapies in sickle cell disease*. Lancet 2002;360:629-631.

26. Ballas SK. *Sickle cell disease: current clinical management*. Seminars in Hematology 2001;38:307-314.

27. The Coroner's Autopsy: Do we deserve better? National Confidential Enquiry into Patient Outcome and Death. 2006. *www.ncepod.org.uk*

2 – Study methods

Study aim

The primary aim of this study was to collect information on the care received by haemoglobinopathy patients who died in England, Wales, Northern Ireland, Isle of Man, Guernsey and Jersey in order to identify remediable factors in the care of these patients.

The secondary aims were to document the causes of death among children and adults with sickle cell diseases and thalassaemia; and to evaluate how well autopsies on these patients were performed.

Areas of interest

At the start of the study there were no generic guidelines for the management of haemoglobinopathy patients in the UK. The only national guidelines (as opposed to individual hospitals' protocols) were those on managing acute painful crisis [1]. Prior to the commencement of data collection an expert group met to determine the key areas of interest in the study. It was decided that the study should collect information on the following:

1. Outpatient care
   * Regular participation in outpatient clinics
   * Regular management received and its appropriateness
   * Level of involvement of GP in care loop
   * Reluctance of patients to attend hospital.

2. Pain management
   * Management of sickle pain
   * Pain services' level of understanding of managing sickle pain
   * Vulnerability to escalations in dose
   * Appropriateness of pain management.

3. Mortality associated with surgery
   * Appropriateness of peri-operative care
   * Factors influencing outcome.

4. Experience of managing haemoglobinopathies
   * Level of experience, grades and specialties of doctors and nurses managing patients.

5. Clinical pathology
   * Patterns of fatal clinical pathology
   * Quality of autopsy reports and cause of death formulations.

6. Organisation and provision of care
   * Availability of hospital protocols for management of patients
   * Inter-hospital protocols
   * Organisation of regional specialist centres
   * Regional centres' protocols.

7. National guidelines
   * Review locally available and national guidelines.

Expert group

A group of experts comprising haematologists, a haemoglobinopathy nurse specialist, an anaesthetist, paediatricians, a pathologist, a patient representative and a Sickle Cell Society representative contributed to the design of the study and the questionnaires. They also reviewed the combined analysis of the data from both the questionnaires and the information from the advisor groups.

Study design

The study was conducted using both qualitative and quantitative methods of data collection from a selected group of patients. Peer review of each case was undertaken to identify possible remediable factors in the care of these patients.

Sample selection

The expert group proposed that the study should include both sickle cell disease and thalassaemia patients, to allow creation of a complete picture of the provision of care for haemoglobinopathy patients. All patients who died with sickle cell disease (ICD-10 code D57) or thalassaemia (ICD-10 code D56) recorded anywhere in their diagnosis or cause of death were included.

Patients with the following haemoglobinopathies were included:
- Sickle cell anaemia (HbSS)
- Sickle haemoglobin C (HbSC)
- Sickle haemoglobin D (HbSD)
- Sickle ß-thalassaemia (HbS ß-Thal)
- ß-thalassaemia major
- ß-thalassaemia intermedia.

National data for three years preceding commencement of the study suggested that there were between 40-50 deaths annually of these patients. A long data collection period was, therefore, required to obtain sufficient data. Data were collected over a period of two years (1st January 2005 – 31st December 2006).

Data were collected on both adults and children. Both hospital and community deaths were included.

Exclusions

The following two groups of patients were excluded from the study:
- Patients with sickle and thalassaemia traits and no relevant clinical symptoms (including both clinician and advisors' opinion)
- Patients who died abroad.

Hospital participation

All relevant National Health Service Hospitals in England, Wales and Northern Ireland were expected to participate, as well as all relevant hospitals in the independent sector and public hospitals in the Isle of Man, Guernsey and Jersey.

Within each site, a named contact, referred to as the NCEPOD Local Reporter, acted as a liaison between NCEPOD and the hospital, facilitating data collection and dissemination of questionnaires.

Case ascertainment

A number of different data collection methods were used in order to identify as many patients as possible:

1. **NCEPOD Local Reporters**
   NCEPOD has a contact in each hospital known as a Local Reporter. In this study, the Local Reporter was responsible for searching the patient administration system for any patients with ICD-10 codes D56 and D57 anywhere in their diagnosis or cause of death. Patients were then reported by means of a password protected spreadsheet. Nil returns were also requested for hospitals where there were no patients identified in the timeframe.

2. **Specialist centres**
   A contact was identified in each of the sickle cell and thalassaemia specialist centres. This contact acted like a Local Reporter for the study and returned data on a six-monthly basis.

3. **Specialist clinicians**
   Specialist clinicians were made aware of the study and its progress via the UK Forum on Haemoglobin Disorders and the NCEPOD website. They were able to report cases directly to NCEPOD via a downloadable form on the NCEPOD website.

4. **Office for National Statistics (ONS)**
   NCEPOD received a report of deaths of haemoglobinopathy patients in hospitals and the community on a six-monthly basis.

5. **General Practitioners (GPs)**
   The study was publicised via GP bulletins at the start of the data collection period. GPs were able to report cases directly to NCEPOD. No reports were received via this route.

Questionnaires and casenotes

For each case reported, a questionnaire was sent out retrospectively. Each questionnaire comprised three sections:
1. The patient's regular haemoglobinopathy management
2. Final clinical episode
3. Organisation of care

For patients who died in hospital, the questionnaire was sent to the inpatient consultant responsible for managing the patient's haemoglobinopathy during their final admission.

For those patients who died in the community, the questionnaire was sent to the last GP surgery or specialist centre at which the patient was managed.

For those patients who died at centres other than their regular management unit, section 1 was completed by the healthcare professional responsible for the patient's regular management and sections 2 and 3 by the clinician responsible for managing the patient at the time of death.

The last six months of the patient's casenotes were requested. This included medical notes, nursing notes and GP/specialist centre notes. Any referral letters, fluid balance charts and temperature, pulse and respiration (TPR) charts were also requested. If available, a copy of the autopsy report was also requested. At an organisational level, copies of protocols were also collected.

Advisor group

A multidisciplinary group of advisors was selected to review the questionnaires and casenotes. The group of advisors comprised a haematologist, a paediatric haematologist, a haemoglobinopathy nurse, an anaesthetist/pain specialist and a pathologist.

For each case reviewed, the advisors completed an assessment form. This allowed both quantitative and qualitative analysis of the advisors' opinions.

Peer review process

All questionnaires and casenotes were anonymised by the research staff at NCEPOD. All identifiable details relating to the patient, medical staff and hospital were removed. No clinical staff at NCEPOD, nor the advisors, had access to any information that would allow individuals to be identified.

Following anonymisation, each case was reviewed by two of the advisors independently. The cases were often very complex and review by two advisors allowed the process to be as thorough as possible. At regular intervals throughout the meeting, the chair facilitated discussion of themes or areas of concern.

Data analysis

All data were analysed using Microsoft Access and Excel, within the NCEPOD offices, by the NCEPOD research staff.

The findings of the report were reviewed by the expert group, advisors and the NCEPOD Steering Group prior to publication.

Quality and confidentiality

Questionnaires were checked on return to NCEPOD and if any key data were missing this was followed up, to allow data analysis to be performed effectively. Missing casenotes that were essential to the peer review process, including fluid balance charts and autopsy reports, were also followed up if not returned to NCEPOD.

Once the questionnaires were as complete as possible, the identifying casenote number (and any other identifiable information) on each questionnaire was removed.

The data from all the questionnaires and assessment forms were electronically scanned into a preset database. Prior to any analysis taking place, the dataset was cleaned to ensure that there were no duplicate records and that erroneous data had not been entered during scanning. All data were then validated by the NCEPOD research staff.

Reference

1. Rees DC, Olujohungbe AD, Parker NE *et al. Guidelines for the management of the acute painful crisis in sickle cell disease.* British Journal of Haematology 2003;120:744-52.

3 – Overview of data collected

Number of cases

Figure 1 shows that 174 cases were identified via the various methods of reporting for inclusion in the study. Of these cases, 93 were subsequently excluded. Cases were mainly excluded upon review by clinicians and considered to have an asymptomatic trait. In a number of cases, the casenotes and completed questionnaires were returned to NCEPOD and the case excluded by the advisors.

Of the 81 included cases, 47 had both casenotes and a questionnaire returned and a further eight had casenotes but no questionnaire. In total, 55 included cases were assessed by the advisors. Of the 81 included cases, 26 had neither casenotes nor a questionnaire returned and so could not be assessed.

Denominators for this report will either be out of 55 when considering the casenotes or the advisors' opinion or 47 when considering the data returned to NCEPOD by clinicians completing the questionnaire.

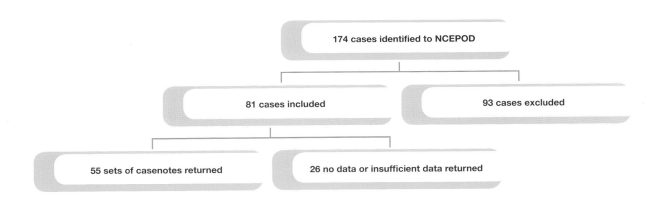

Figure 1. Cases identified

Hospital participation

Of 1042 open sites, 653 (63%) returned data for the study. The return rate amongst the acute sites was higher. 76% of acute sites (500/654) returned data for at least one month of the study.

Method of reporting

Cases were reported via a number of methods as outlined in the methods section. However, almost half of included patients were reported only by the NCEPOD Local Reporter. A further 27 patients were reported by two or more methods. There were no patients reported directly by a GP. These data can be seen in Figure 2.

Age at diagnosis

The clinician completing the questionnaire was asked for the age at which the patient was diagnosed with a haemoglobinopathy. Table 1 shows that five patients were diagnosed at birth; of these three were still paediatric cases at death. The number of patients diagnosed later in life is likely to decrease following the rollout of the Newborn Screening Programme nationally, although immigrant patients will continue to present later.

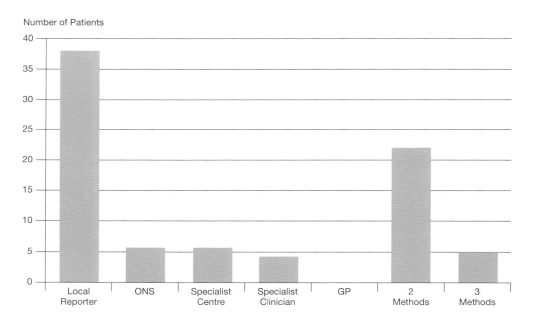

Figure 2. Method of reporting included patients

Number of Patients

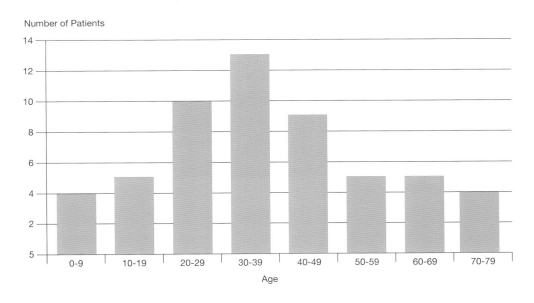

Figure 3. Age of haemoglobinopathy patients at death

Table 1. Age at diagnosis

Age at diagnosis	Number of patients
At birth	5
Aged 0-10 years	6
Aged 20+ years	7
Unknown	20
Not answered	9
Total	47

Age and gender of patients

Thirty-one patients in the study were male. The age range of patients was 1 to 77 years old. There were six paediatric cases (<16 years of age). The paediatric cases are discussed in more detail later in the report.

The modal age bracket was 30-39 years of age (Figure 3). These patients were born just before or at the start of the 1970s, which coincided with changes in the management of these patients; notably the use of penicillin prophylaxis. The median survival in 1994 was 42 years for males and 48 years for females [1]. Now >90% of identified children with sickle cell disease are expected to achieve adulthood [2].

Type of haemoglobinopathy

Table 2. Type of haemoglobinopathy

Type of haemoglobinopathy	Number of patients
HbSS	32
HbSC	11
HbSD	0
Sickle cell trait	2
HbS ß-Thal	3
ß-Thalassaemia major	4
ß-Thalassaemia intermedia	3
Total	**55**

HbSS was the most common genotype in the study. For every three patients with HbSS, there was one patient with HbSC included. This 3:1 ratio is in line with the genotypes identified nationally in the Newborn Screening Programme [3]. Although there are often fewer symptoms in HbSC patients, it is not necessarily less severe. HbSC is increasing in the UK population and it can be considered the most treacherous form of sickle cell disease as it is easy to misjudge the risks to the patient.

As mentioned previously, a large number of patients reported to NCEPOD were excluded as they had asymptomatic traits. However, the clinicians and advisors believed that in two cases the patient's sickle cell trait was relevant to the cause of the patient's death. These will be discussed later in the report (see 'Main patterns of death' p.25).

Table 3. Place of death

Place of death	Number of patients
Hospital	41
Community	11
Community following hospital discharge	3
Total	**55**

Place of death

Hospital deaths were the most common, with 41 of 55 patients dying in hospital (Table 3). Fourteen patients died in the community; three of these within 14 days of discharge from hospital (of these three, the cause of death was not known in two, so comment on post-discharge morbidity and mortality was not possible).

Final clinical episode

Time of admission

Figure 4 demonstrates the time of admission. Of the 41 patients who died in hospital, 17 were admitted in working hours (08:00 -17:59) and 14 were admitted out of hours (18:00 – 07:59). In ten cases, the time of admission was not documented in the notes.

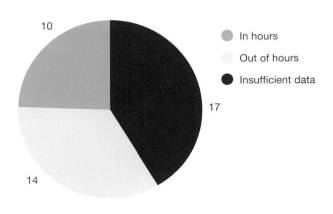

10

In hours
Out of hours
Insufficient data

17

14

Figure 4. Time of admission

Number of days spent in hospital

More than half of the patients (21/41) who died in hospital only spent between 0 and 5 days in hospital in their final episode (Figure 5). However, three patients spent 26 or more days in hospital; the longest being 117 days.

Main patterns of death

The information available for review by the study advisors included hospital records, clinician statements and some autopsy reports. As with previous NCEPOD reviews, significant disagreements arose over the actual causes of death and the co-morbidities as submitted and as interpreted by the advisors (this is addressed in 'Death certification and autopsies'). In several cases, there was no evident cause of death (either not submitted, or the advisors could come to no definite conclusion). For the remainder, the causes of death and co-morbidities are the consensus opinion of the advisors.

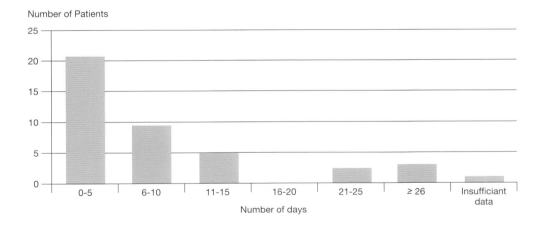

Number of Patients

Figure 5. Number of days spent in hospital

Sickle cell and thalassaemia traits

A substantial number of cases were sent to NCEPOD for review where the underlying haemoglobinopathy was sickle cell trait (HbAS) or thalassaemia trait. Although the study was not set up to review the understanding of the heterozygous states for haemoglobinopathies, it was obvious from the frequency with which this irrelevant data was entered on to death certificates that many doctors were not aware of the clinical consequences of these conditions or not aware of how to fill in a death certificate. In one case, a very eldery patient with thalassaemia trait had thalassaemia listed in part 2 of their death certificate. This demonstrated a potential lack of understanding on the part of the doctor completing the death certificate for this patient, who in fact died of cancer. The majority of people with thalassaemia trait will never suffer any consequences of their genetic inheritance, and none were evident from this study.

People with sickle cell trait may develop problems under extreme circumstances; it is known that army recruits with sickle cell trait are more likely to die in training than their peers during intensive exercises and if these patients are rendered hypoxic, for example during anaesthesia, there could be problems [4]. However, for all but two of the cases referred to us the carrier status was of no consequence.

One case of metastatic renal medullary carcinoma described below was appropriately linked to sickle cell trait.

CASE STUDY 1

A young patient with sickle cell trait presented with haematuria and other kidney problems. Investigations showed that they had metastatic renal medullary carcinoma. The patient subsequently died.

The advisors were of the view that this rare type of renal carcinoma is virtually restricted to those with the sickle gene, particularly sickle trait (HbAS), HbSC and occasionally HbSS [5]. The prognosis for this carcinoma is very poor, and survival is less than one year from diagnosis [6].

The second case in which the advisors believed that sickle cell trait contributed to death was previously asymptomatic.

CAS STUDY 2

An elderly female, known to be HbAS but previously asymptomatic, developed post-menopausal bleeding and had an endoscopic uterine polypectomy. Discharged home the next day, she was re-admitted a day later, collapsed and in multi-organ failure. Streptococcal sepsis was diagnosed microbiologically and she died three days post-polypectomy on the ICU. The original coronial autopsy diagnosis, where the pathologist did not know of the bacteraemia, was:

1a. Acute renal tubular necrosis

1b. Sickle cell crisis

Following expert review of the histopathology, at Inquest, the diagnosis was changed to:

1a. Multi-organ failure

1b. Streptococcal sepsis and sickle crisis

1c. Uterine polyp (operated on xx/xx/xxxx)

2. Sickle cell trait

The advisors believed that the severe sequestration of red sickle cells in the lungs, as a result of infection, was considered to have contributed to the death.

Thalassaemia

Seven patients with thalassaemia died; three with thalassasemia intermedia (age range 39-58 years) and four with thalassasemia major (age range 19-32 years). Only two of the seven patients – both with thalassaemia major - were judged to have died of complications related to thalassaemia; one with cardiomyopathy and the other with mucormycosis (diabetes, presumably haemosiderotic, being a co-morbidity). The other five patients died of cirrhosis (n=2; one known to be Hepatitis C virus-related), carcinoma of the lung, possible sepsis (but difficult to determine from the records) and one with no cause of death provided.

Larger studies of thalassaemia mortality, from Cyprus and Italy, emphasise cardiac failure as the single commonest pathogenesis [7, 8], along with liver disease and infection.

The sickle cell diseases

The remaining patients (n=46) were subdivided into paediatric (<16 years) and adults (16 and more years).

Paediatric patients

There were six children (age range 1-15 years). The two youngest (age 1-2 years) both had significant non-sickle co-morbidities: severe prematurity and complications, and an unidentified neuromuscular degeneration respectively. These two cases were not considered further for this study's purposes and there were no indications of substandard care.

Of the four other children, a two-year old died of pneumococcal sepsis and crisis, and one child (4 years) had no given cause of death. Two older children died of cerebrovascular events diagnosed as subarachnoid haemorrhage; neither had an autopsy. Thus no paediatric patients definitely had an ischaemic stroke.

From this small sample, the causes of death are fairly typical for patients of this age.

Adults

There were 40 adults (age range 16-74 years) with the phenotypes HbSS (28), HbSC (10) and HbS-ß-thalassasemia (2). The main cause of death for these patients is illustrated in table 4.

Table 4. Causes of death of adult sickle cell disease patients

Stroke	7	Cirrhosis	2
Haemorrhagic	5	Pulmonary embolism	2
Ischaemic	0	Pulmonary fibrosis	1
Cerebrovascular event undefined	2	Haemosiderotic heart failure	1
		Post-operative haemorrhage	1
Multi-organ failure	3	Renal failure	2
Sepsis	1	Diabetes	1
Pneumonia	1	Cancer	4
Pulmonary hypertension	1	Systemic lupus erythematosus (SLE)	2
		HIV	1
Acute chest syndrome	2	Unknown (Of whom 3 were deaths in the community and no further information obtained)	11
With proven sepsis	1		
With pulmonary hypertension	1		

Among the unknown causes of death were two where opioid toxicity could not be excluded. Comments on the autopsy process are made later in the report (Chapter 8).

Thus, stroke was the single commonest cause of death in adults. All the indicated underlying causes (none confirmed at autopsy) were haemorrhagic. None were ischaemic. One of the haemorrhagic strokes was demonstrated to be associated with arterial aneurysm. The next commonest scenario was combinations of acute chest syndrome, sepsis and multi-organ failure.

The syndrome of multi-organ failure in sickle cell disease has been well recognised as part of the sickle crisis phenomenon. Painful crisis is often a precipitator, and sepsis is not necessarily part of the pathogenesis [9, 10].

There was only one post-operative death clearly identified in the reported patients with sickle cell disease: intra-abdominal haemorrhage following laparoscopic cholecystectomy (case discussed in 'Final Clinical Management' chapter). In another case, where the questionnaire indicated death from intestinal adhesions, the cause could not be resolved by the advisors.

In 8/29 cases where the cause of death was agreed amongst the advisors, the cause was unrelated to sickle cell disease, with cancer predominating (two lung cancers, one myeloma and one astrocytoma).

The subset of Sickle haemoglobin C (HbSC) patients

The ten adult patients with HbSC who died had an age range of 26-74; median 45 years. For the oldest, no cause of death was ascertainable from the information provided. Only two of the ten patients had deaths that could be directly attributed to sickle cell disease (intracerebral haemorrhage and pulmonary embolism), whilst five died primarily of unrelated diseases (brain tumour; diabetes; advanced HIV disease; and two with severe systemic lupus erythematosus).

Patients with HbSC have fewer symptoms from sickle cell disease compared with those having the HbSS phenotype [11]. The presence of co-morbidities such as hypertension, diabetes and obesity in HbSC patients, along with the relatively late age (50 years median) at presentation with sickle-related disease has previously been emphasised [12].

Two of the ten HbSC patients died with systemic lupus erythematosus. Whether this was co-incidental or there was a pathogenetic association could be investigated further in cohorts of patients with this haemoglobinopathy.

Overall standard of care

The NCEPOD grading system for overall standard of care is outlined below. Care was graded by the advisors and ranged from good practice to less than satisfactory, with various grades for room for improvement in between.

NCEPOD grading of care

Good practice: A standard that you would accept from yourself, your trainees and your institution.
Room for improvement: Aspects of *clinical care* that could have been better.
Room for improvement: Aspects of *organisational care* that could have been better.
Room for improvement: Aspects of both *clinical care* and *organisational care* that could have been better.
Less than satisfactory: Several aspects of *clinical* and/or *organisational care* that were well below satisfactory.
Insufficient information: Insufficient information available to assess the quality of care.
Not applicable: No known ongoing care.

This study sought information about the regular ongoing care of haemoglobinopathy patients, as well as the events surrounding their deaths (see Final Clinical Management, chapter 6). This ongoing care may be shared across general practitioners, sickle cell centres and hospital clinics. It includes pain relief (see Pain Management chapter 5), prophylactic therapy, transfusion, vaccination, chelation therapy, renal dialysis and other appropriate day-case interventions. The advisors were, therefore, asked to grade the ongoing care and final clinical episode care separately.

It might appear from the data in the Tables 5 and 6 that the long term management of patients is superior to that during the final clinical episodes. However, by the nature of the study – selecting for death – it is likely that the care in the episode preceding death will appear to be suboptimal (because they died). This is not necessarily the case. Nonetheless, there are several aspects that emerged where improvements could be made and these will be discussed throughout this report.

Table 5. Overall assessment – ongoing care

Overall assessment	Total
Good practice	23
Room for improvement - clinical	8
Room for improvement - organisational	0
Room for improvement - clinical & organisational	2
Less than satisfactory	3
Insufficient information	16
Not applicable	3
Grand Total	**55**

Table 6. Overall assessment – final clinical episode

Overall assessment	Total
Good practice	17
Room for improvement - clinical	14
Room for improvement - organisational	1
Room for improvement - clinical & organisational	1
Less than satisfactory	7
Insufficient information	1
Grand Total	**41**

Key Finding

- A disproportionately large number of cases with thalassaemia and sickle cell disease trait were reported to NCEPOD when the trait was not relevant.

Recommendations

- In our multi-racial society, it is essential that all doctors should have a basic understanding of the implications of thalassaemia and sickle cell trait. (General Medical Council)

- Sickle cell trait and thalassaemia trait should rarely be included on the death certificate; and if included this should only be after review by an individual who has experience in haemoglobinopathies. (Pathologists)

References

1. Platt OS, Brambilla DJ, Rosse WF *et al. Mortality in sickle cell disease. Life expectancy and risk factors for early death*. NEJM 1994;330(23):1639-44

2. Telfer P, Coen P, Chakravorty S *et al. Clinical outcomes in children with sickle cell disease living in England: a neonatal cohort in East London*. Haematologica 2007;92:905-921.

3. Newborn Screening Programme. *http://www.kcl-phs.org.uk/haemscreening/newborn.htm*

4. Kark JA, Posey DM, Schumacher HR *et al. Sickle cell trait as a risk factor for sudden death in physical training*. NEJM 1987;78:890-1.

5. Dimashkieh H, Choe J, Mutema G. *Renal medullar carcinoma: a report of 2 cases and review of the literature*. Archives of Pathology and Laboratory Medicine 2003;127:135-8.

6. Watanabe IC, Billis A, Guimarães MS *et al. Renal medullary carcinoma: a report of seven cases from Brazil*. Modern Pathology 2007:20:914-20.

7. Telfer P, Coen PG, Christou S *et al. Survival of medically treated thalassaemia patients in Cyprus. Trends and risks factors over the period 1980-2004*. Haematologica 2006;91:1187-92.

8. Borgna-Pignatti C, Rugolotto S, De Stefano P *et al. Survival and complications in patients with thalassemia major treated with transfusion and deferoxamine*. Haematologica 2004;89(10):1187-93.

9. Hassell KL, Eckman JR, Lane PA. *Acute multi-organ failure syndrome: a potentially catastrophic complication of severe sickle cell pain episodes*. American Journal of Medicine 1994;96:155-62.

10. Hiran S. *Multi-organ dysfunction syndrome in sickle cell disease*. Journal of the Associations of Physicians of India 2005;53:19-22.

11. Serjeant GR, Serjeant BE. *Sickle Cell Disease*, 3rd edn, Oxford University Press, Oxford, 2001.

12. Koduri PR, Agbemadzo B, Nathan S. *Hemoglobin SC disease revisited: clinical study of 106 adults*. American Journal of Hematology 2001;68:298-300.

4 – Ongoing care

Introduction

This chapter describes the care received by haemoglobinopathy patients from their general practitioners (GPs) and hospital sickle clinics as part of their long term disease management. The last six months of casenotes were requested for each patient included in the study.

The Department of Health has issued guidance on the management of hyposplenism, with reference to preventing infections [1]. That aside, there were not yet any other official British/NHS guidance documents providing standards of regular care.

The advisors could not tell from this study whether all patients with haemoglobinopathy were being cared for regularly. Whilst all screen positive children are offered appointments for haemoglobinopathy clinics, it is anecdotally likely that a proportion of undiagnosed adults are unknown to the medical care systems.

Regular medications

Of the 47 patients for whom a questionnaire was returned, 16 patients received transfusions. Of these, 11 patients had sickle cell disease and five had thalassaemia. Twenty patients were receiving folic acid and six hydroxycarbamide. Fourteen patients were reported by clinicians to be receiving regular pain medication. The use of pain medication in the ongoing management of these patients is discussed in the following chapter.

Antibiotic prophylaxis

Seventeen patients were taking prophylactic antibiotics. There is clear evidence of the benefit of antibiotic prophylaxis in children with sickle cell disease [2,3]. In adults the benefit is less certain. In the one case of death in childhood from streptococcal sepsis, no vaccination or prophylaxis had been administered, despite being offered.

Vaccinations

The uptake of vaccinations by sickle cell patients in the GP setting was very low in this study. Untreated sickle cell disease patients have a 250 fold increase of infection (particularly pneumococcal) [4-7] than the general population, so vaccination is of increased importance [8]. Pneumococcal vaccination and annual influenza vaccination are increasingly offered to all patients with HbSS, and many with HbSC, in line with the hyposplenism guidelines.

As illustrated in Figure 6, pneumococcal vaccine had the highest uptake. The clinicians managing these patients only reported 15/47 as having received this vaccine. Annual influenza vaccination had a particularly low uptake, with only three patients known to have been vaccinated.

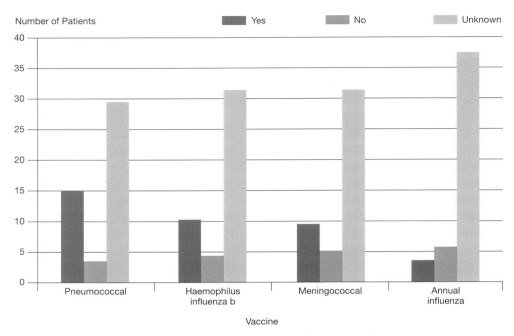

Figure 6. Vaccinations received by the patient

Location of patient management

The management of haemoglobinopathy patients is often split among different sites and centres. Specialist centres have an important part to play in the management of these patients. Twenty five patients were managed at a specialist centre (Figure 7). Eleven patients were managed at two or more different units.

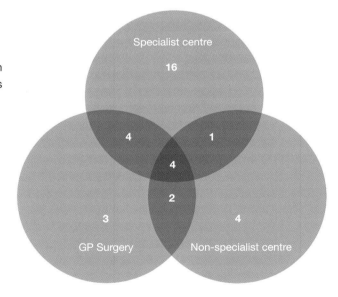

Figure 7. Location of where patients were managed

Outpatient appointments

Two thirds of patients (28/47) attended outpatients, with varying degrees of regularity (Figure 8).

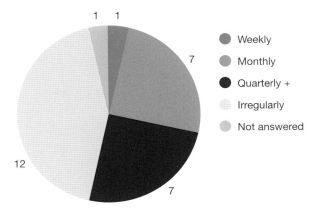

Figure 8. Regular attendance at outpatients

Twelve patients who attended outpatient appointments were reported by the clinicians to do so irregularly (Figure 8). On analysis of the patient casenotes, the advisors considered 11/55 patients to have shown a reluctance to attend appointments. Of the 11 patients who showed a reluctance to attend outpatients, in four cases the advisors' judged that this may have had an impact on patient outcome. In a further three cases there was insufficient information to comment (Figure 9).

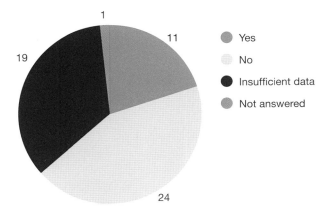

Figure 9. Reluctance to attend appointments

Medical advice and treatment

There were 14 patients who were considered not to have taken medical advice or to have refused treatment as shown in Figure 10. In eight of these cases, the advisors judged that this could have had an impact on patient care. In a further two cases, there was insufficient information for the advisors to make a judgement.

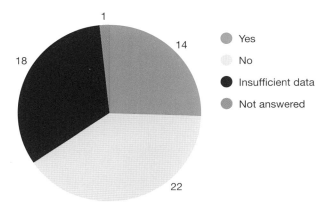

Figure 10. Refusal to accept medical advice/treatment

Patients have the right to refuse treatment; there were examples of this right being exercised in a positive way with clear communication between the patient and the team offering care.

Some problems, most notably iron overload, develop over a period of years and because this study only examined the records for the last six months of the patient's life it was not always possible to make a judgement as to the reasons for refusal of treatment. This is exemplified in case study 3.

CASE STUDY 3

A young patient with thalassaemia was known to have severe iron overload with a ferritin that was persistently above the target range. Offers were made to increase the iron chelation therapy, but this change was not implemented. The likeliest cause of death was cardiac iron overload.

Whilst the advisors believed that the offers to increase iron chelation might have helped, the problem must have arisen over a period of many years and the advisors could not assess whether the patient had appropriate psychological and other support.

Regular attenders

Due to the nature of the disease, a subset of sickle cell disease patients regularly attend hospital. These patients are often referred to as regular attenders. This group of patients poses a different set of management problems to those patients who present infrequently. In patients who are regularly in and out of hospital, there is the possibility of healthcare professionals becoming complacent with regards to the management of these patients. It is paramount that the healthcare professionals listen to the patients. The patients are aware of their usual patterns of crisis and if they say that the pain is different, this should be acted upon. Healthcare professionals should also be careful not to underestimate the severity of non-sickle complications in regular attenders.

CASE STUDY 4

A middle-aged patient with HbSS disease presented, one month prior to final admission and death, with left sided chest pain radiating to the left neck. The patient stated that the pain "felt different to the sickle pain" and there was no relief from taking paracetamol. There was no indication of acute chest syndrome or ischaemic heart disease. The patient was discharged, but was re-admitted unconscious with a stroke. Investigations revealed a subarachnoid haemorrhage associated with a berry aneurysm of the left anterior communicating artery and a tortuous left internal carotid artery.

The advisors believed it possible that the unusual pain was a prodrome for the progression of the cranial artery disease. It may have made no difference in this particular case, but clinicians should note what the patient says about their symptoms.

Recommendations

- As a minimum, the Department of Health guidance regarding vaccination and prophylactic antibiotics should be followed in order to prevent sepsis from hyposplenism. (Primary Care Trusts)

- All children with sickle cell disease should receive pneumococcal vaccination according to national guidance and regular penicillin prophylaxis from the age of three months. Regular review in a specialist centre is advised. (Primary Care Trusts)

- Patients should be encouraged to understand the importance of regular review to optimise the management of their condition. (Primary and Secondary Care Trusts)

- There needs to be clear recording of vaccination status to prevent omission by default; liaison between primary and secondary care is needed. (Primary and Secondary Care Trusts)

References

1. Splenectomy: Information for patients and patient card.
   http://www.dh.gov.uk/en/Publicationsandstatistics/Publications/PublicationsPolicyAndGuidance/DH_4113581

2. Newborn Screening Programme.
   http://www.kcl-phs.org.uk/haemscreening/newborn.htm

3. Dick M. Sickle Cell Disease in Childhood, Standards and Guidelines in Clinical Care. For the UK Forum on Haemoglobin Disorders. NHS Sickle Cell and Thalassaemia Screening Programme in partnership with the Sickle Cell Society 2006.

4. Riddington C, Owusu-Ofori S. *Prophylactic antibiotics for preventing pneumococcal infection in children with sickle cell disease*. Cochrane Database Syst Rev. 2002;(3):CD003427.

5. Raghavan M, Davies SC. *The management of haemoglobinopathies*. Curr Paediatr 20002; 12:290-297

6. Landesman SH, Rao SP, Ahonkhai VI. *Infections in children with sickle cell anaemia. Special reference to pneumococcal and salmonella infections*. Am J Pediatr Haematol Oncol 1982;4(4):407-8

7. Wong WY, Overturf GD, Powars DR. *Infection caused by Streptococcus pneumonia in children with sickle cell disease: epidemiology, immunological mechanisms, prophylaxis, and vaccination*. Clin Infect Dis 1992;14:1124-36.

8. Important changes to childhood immunisation. CMO, 2006

5 – Pain management

Introduction

Pain is the most frequent problem experienced by individuals who have sickle cell disease and has a major impact on their quality of life [1]. The complexity of this pain poses significant challenges for those who have sickle cell disease, as well as the healthcare professionals who care for them. The extent, intensity and frequency of the pain are hugely variable between individuals. Many patients have underlying chronic pain accompanied by superimposed acute pain episodes which may be unpredictable in onset and duration.

The management and control of pain associated with sickle cell disease is complicated by many factors including cultural beliefs, misconceptions and perceived or real inequalities of access to health care. An example of how these can affect patient care is in relation to drug dependency. There was agreement between the NCEPOD expert sickle cell group that people with sickle cell disease are more likely to abuse opioid analgesics and other drugs. This can cause barriers to adequate pain management. Consequently, ensuring an understanding relationship between healthcare professionals and patients with sickle cell disease is essential in providing pain control care which is tailored to individual patients' needs. This can be best achieved by healthcare professionals working in partnership with patients to develop pain management strategies [1].

For the deaths reported to NCEPOD, information was sought on ongoing pain management as well as the acute management of pain during the patient's final episode in hospital.

Ongoing pain management

Clinicians completing the questionnaire were asked to provide information on the type and frequency of use of analgesics taken by patients for their ongoing pain management. Furthermore, the advisors were asked to give their opinion of the management of long term pain control and drug dependency issues.

A questionnaire was returned for 40 of the 48 sickle cell disease patients. Of these, 14 were reported by clinicians to be taking regular analgesic medications for ongoing pain management. The most commonly used non-opioid analgesics were paracetamol (8) and NSAIDs (8). All of these patients also took opioid analgesics including codeine phosphate, dihydrocodeine, morphine and pethidine. In only one patient was there evidence of medication being dispensed from multiple sources.

In the opinion of the advisors, in six patients there was evidence of dependency issues. However, in a further 13 patients there was insufficient information from the casenotes to form an opinion.

Of the six patients who were thought to have drug dependency issues, three had multiple hospital attendances requesting opioid analgesia; one of them became aggressive when these requests were refused. One patient had sufficient medical problems that would explain significant chronic pain. However, the advisors considered that they were taking excessive quantities of opioids including buprenorphine via both transdermal patch and sublingually, plus oral morphine and subcutaneous diamorphine.

A further patient was receiving oral pethidine and fentanyl patches on a regular basis between crises, which was considered unusual by the advisors (and there have been occasional reports of fatality from fentanyl patch overdose [2]). And another patient was taking very high doses of opioids between painful crises.

In four of these patients with drug dependency problems, the advisors found evidence that the clinicians who cared for them had explored this aspect of care. For one patient there were insufficient data. The advisors commented that in one patient the psychology team had informed other hospitals not to duplicate prescriptions. Another patient was referred to a pain clinic, but an additional referral to a psychologist and drug dependency team would have made valuable contributions to this patient's care in the view of the advisors. There was a lack of multidisciplinary care or of a management protocol. However, in another case, there was mention of drug withdrawal and care was taken to record opioid use and to discuss dependency issues with the patient.

In addition, one patient received increasing doses of analgesia and was also considered to have been developing a tolerance to opioids.

The following case study provides examples of some issues described.

CASE STUDY 5

A young patient with sickle cell disease was known to have a drug dependency and was receiving opioids on a regular basis. They sought help from a sickle cell centre. The patient was allowed to leave the clinic before arrangements had been made for them to be seen by a psychologist working for the drug dependency team. The patient did not return to the clinic and their body was discovered some two weeks later.

The advisors believed that having attended the clinic seeking help, the fact that the patient was allowed to leave before support had been organised may have contributed to the subsequent tragic events.

Furthermore, the quality of the autopsy was poor. It is unlikely that the true cause of death will ever be known, but it was noteworthy that "a white substance was found in the stomach and in the trachea". It is most likely that this person had vomited and died from aspiration of vomit. Given the known problems with drug dependency, it was likely that this was directly due to opioid misuse.

Discussion

While the sample of patients included in this study may not be representative of all patients with sickle cell disease, there were examples of both good and poor care relating to ongoing pain management that can provide valuable learning points. The majority of patients assessed by the advisors appeared to receive good ongoing pain management and many patients only required simple analgesia between painful episodes. Of those who did require opioid analgesics, there seems to have been a wide variation in the types and routes of administration both between patients, as well as for the same patient. This may be appropriate, depending on the patient's needs, but the complexities of multiple therapies can make adequate assessment of efficacy of pain treatment difficult.

Furthermore, there was little evidence found of how ongoing pain was assessed in patients. Formalised methods for assessing chronic pain are available and could be adapted for use in patients with sickle cell disease [3]. Clinicians who care for these patients should liaise with their local chronic pain service.

The management of ongoing pain in patients with sickle cell disease can be challenging. This is particularly true in those patients with drug dependency. While there was evidence that clinicians caring for patients included in this study did appreciate these issues, there did not appear to be any formal arrangements between drug dependency teams and haemoglobinopathy clinics. The care of these patients requires a multidisciplinary approach from experts in sickle cell disease, chronic pain and drug dependency. In addition, support groups for patients with sickle cell disease can be invaluable. The development of formal procedures to identify patients with drug dependency problems, their assessment and management would benefit this group of patients.

Acute, final clinical episode, pain management

From the casenotes, the advisors assessed the acute pain management of the sickle cell disease patients who died in hospital. Of the 35 sickle cell disease patients who died in hospital, 19 had pain as an admitting complaint. It had been hoped to determine the time from admission to the first analgesia, but due to poor documentation this was only possible to verify in two patients. Both of these patients received their first analgesia in the emergency department 90 minutes after admission, whereas the current guidelines state that analgesia should be given within 30 minutes of entering the hospital [4].

In only six patients was there evidence in the casenotes that pain was formally assessed using a pain assessment chart. Three of these charts were specifically designed for sickle cell disease patients and included an algorithm for management of painful crisis. The remaining charts were non specific combined temperature, pulse, respiratory rate (TPR) and pain assessment charts. In none of the casenotes reviewed was the frequency of pain assessments specified by the admitting doctor. The advisors judged that the frequency of pain assessments was inadequate based on the severity of pain in five of the six patients where formal assessment of pain was undertaken. Of the remaining 13 patients who complained of pain on admission, where there was no evidence of formal pain assessment, it is possible that formal assessment did take place but the pain charts were not sent to NCEPOD. Even so, in eight of these cases the advisors could not identify any written commentary that regular pain assessment had occurred.

The casenotes were further reviewed for evidence of monitoring of the adverse effects of opioid administration. In six patients, both sedation (using a categorical scale) and respiratory rate were charted. A further eight patients had respiratory rate documented, while in the remaining five patients there was no evidence of any observation being made. In seven patients, the frequency of these documented observations was judged to be inadequate based on the dose of opioids administered. All these patients had escalating doses of opioids.

Furthermore, in nine patients it was the advisors' opinion that excessive doses of opioids had been given and of these there were five patients in whom complications occurred due to opioid overdose. These included respiratory depression and hypotension. It was the advisors' view that these excessive doses contributed to the death of these patients. There was evidence from the casenotes that in seven of the patients who received excessive doses of opioids there was lack of knowledge regarding acute pain management. It was of particular note that in all of these cases, junior trainees were responsible for the prescribing of analgesia and no attempt was made to seek expert advice either from consultants in haemoglobinopathies or acute pain management teams.

The following case studies provide examples of some of these issues.

CASE STUDY 6

A middle aged patient with HbSC disease was admitted in the evening via the emergency department complaining of increasing back and leg pain of 24 hours duration. The patient was not taking any regular analgesia and was initially given diclofenac and co-codamol according to a local sickle cell crisis analgesia regimen. This resulted in minimal improvement in the pain. Following admission, the patient was prescribed 50mg of pethidine IM 4 hourly and later that evening 100mg 2 hourly by a pre-registration house officer. There was no evidence of formal assessment or documentation of pain. Whilst the respiratory rate was documented this was recorded infrequently. In the early evening of the following day, a Senior House Officer (SHO) was asked to insert an intravenous cannula for fluid administration due to poor oral intake in the previous 24 hours. The SHO found the patient unresponsive and despite advanced life support by the cardiac arrest team the patient could not be resuscitated.

The advisors commented that this opioid naïve patient had received 1500mg of pethidine in the 24 hours leading up to their death which was thought to be excessive. The patient should have had more frequent observations of the level of sedation and respiratory rate which reflected the increasing doses of opioids. Furthermore, there was lack of senior medical staff involvement in this patient's care. It was the opinion of the advisors that the opioid overdose was a probable contributing factor to this patient's death which could have been avoided. Despite an autopsy, there was no convincing clinical pathology to account for the death.

CASE STUDY 7

A young adult patient presented to hospital with sickle cell crisis with known documented sensitivity to opioids. The pain was poorly controlled and the patient received increasing doses of opioids, including morphine and pethidine, by a variety of routes of administration. A single observation, recorded two hours before the patient was found arrested, recorded hypotension. Despite this documented deterioration in the patient's clinical condition no apparent action was taken. At least 150mg of morphine had been given in the previous 24 hours.

It was the advisors' view that there had been poor communication between the clinical teams with regard to the known opioid sensitivity of this patient. In addition, there had been a lack of clinical review regarding the increasing analgesic requirements of the patient. The monitoring of vital signs had been inadequate and there had been a failure to take action in response to the deteriorating clinical condition. The advisors were of the opinion that the likely cause of death was opioid overdose and this could have been prevented.

CASE STUDY 8

A young adult presented to the emergency department with HbSS complaining of pain in their arms and legs. They had attended the department the previous day demanding IV morphine which was not given and the patient was sent home. On this second attendance, oral analgesia was refused and again IV morphine was demanded. The patient was described as abusive and aggressive by the medical and nursing staff. Subsequently, the patient was given 20mg of morphine subcutaneously and admitted to the ward. Morphine was given three hourly and was increased to 30mg. During the next six days the patient continued to complain of pain and refused oral and IV fluids. Over this period, it was noted that the patient was becoming increasingly drowsy. A cardiac arrest call was made on day 6 following a grand mal seizure. The patient was given IV diazepam which stopped the seizure, but subsequently had an asystolic cardiac arrest from which they did not recover.

While the advisors accepted that this patient's behaviour made clinical management difficult, why was no action taken regarding the increasing drowsiness? The advisors considered that those healthcare professionals who cared for this patient should have had greater awareness of the complications of opioid overdose and more senior medical advice should have been sought. The overall quality of care was judged to be less than satisfactory.

CASE STUDY 9

A middle aged patient with sickle cell disease was initially seen in a haemoglobinopathy outpatient clinic complaining of a wide variety of painful experiences. Oral morphine was used on a regular basis and the patient was offered an appointment with a clinical psychologist to discuss their use of opioids. The appointment was not attended. The patient was then admitted to hospital ten days later complaining of back pain and remained in hospital for two months before death. The cause of death was unclear because no autopsy was performed. However, during the admission the patient had received a wide range of analgesics including pethidine, morphine and diamorphine via various routes. They had also received an intravenous infusion of midazolam to control agitation.

The advisors remarked that in view of the known problems the patient had experienced with opioids the patient should have been reviewed by a specialist pain team (during their admission). While the cause of death may not have been directly related to the opioid administration, the advisors formed the opinion that this may have been a contributing factor.

Discussion

Management of acute painful episodes is a significant challenge and requires expert knowledge of acute pain management and sickle cell disease by doctors and nurses. National guidelines for acute painful crisis for patients with sickle cell disease have been published and should form the basis for all those caring for these patients [4].

It was of considerable note that in the patients included in this study, basic information on analgesic history, regular pain assessment and assessment of opioid adverse effects, such as sedation scoring and respiratory rate, were rarely documented. Even when this information was recorded it was often not acted upon, resulting in complications that were avoidable. The adequate management of pain can only be effectively achieved by assessing pain at regular intervals based on its severity and using treatments that match these requirements and that are titrated to effect. Simultaneous assessment and measurement of physiological parameters which may indicate adverse effects of opioid analgesics need to be recorded and documented. Trends in analgesic requirements should also be recorded. This information needs to be reviewed regularly to ensure adequate pain control and allow recognition of opioid overdose. The development of "track & trigger" systems would greatly enhance better pain control and patient safety [5].

Two patients presented with severe pain and did not receive treatment in a timely fashion in line with the British Journal of Haematology guidelines [4]. This resulted in patients suffering unnecessarily. Early intervention following admission to hospital to control pain is essential and the use of protocols for the rapid assessment and treatment of pain would aid management. Those patients who have regular painful episodes should have personalised pain control protocols which can allow fast track treatment if admission proves necessary. Patients should be encouraged to be an equal partner in the drawing up of these documents. Consequently, educating patients on strategies to manage their pain should be an important component in this partnership. Indeed, in some circumstances it may be possible to avoid hospital admission as part of these strategies.

There were several patients identified in this study who had escalating opioid requirements which were not recognised as significant by the attending medical and nursing staff. This phenomenon can be an ominous sign of specific medical complications of sickle cell disease such as acute chest syndrome. There were examples of lack of adequate review by attending staff which resulted in unrecognised progressive patient deterioration. In some instances, multiple types of opioids were administered using a variety of routes. There was a perception by the advisors that this was frequently undertaken in desperation because of failing pain control without following a logical clinical approach. Of particular note was the continued use of high dose intramuscular pethidine which is known to have significant adverse effects and has no advantage over morphine [6].

There was a subgroup of patients in whom the advisors believed that adequate pain control may not be achieved despite very high opioid doses. In these circumstances alternative pain therapies, for example regional blockade, may be required and even then adequate pain control may not be possible. These patients require the special attention of experts in pain management, including psychological support.

A recurring theme was the lack of a multidisciplinary approach to acute pain management of patients with a painful crisis. While many of these patients can be managed with standard methods of pain control, involvement of experts in sickle cell disease and acute pain management should be sought if these methods do not adequately control pain. These patients require regular reviews to determine the efficacy of the pain therapy. Furthermore, these multidisciplinary teams can develop local written protocols for the management of painful episodes based on the national guidelines and local facilities. They should provide education and training for both medical and nursing staff who care for sickle cell disease patients.

Key Findings

- Of the 40 sickle cell disease patients for whom a questionnaire was received, 14 took regular pain medications for ongoing pain management. All of these took a combination of opioids and simple analgesics. In only one patient was there was evidence of medication being dispensed from multiple sources.

- In the opinion of the advisors, in six patients there was evidence of dependency issues. However, in 13 patients there was insufficient information from the casenotes to form an opinion.

- In general, there was a lack of a multidisciplinary or multi-agency approach to the management of opioid dependency in these sickle cell disease patients.

- Of the 35 sickle cell disease patients who died in hospital, 19 had pain as an admitting complaint. In nine of these patients, it was the advisors' opinion that excessive doses of opioids had been given and of these there were five patients where complications occurred due to overdose which contributed to the ultimate death of these patients.

- In two thirds of the patients admitted with acute pain there was lack of evidence that pain or the adverse effects of opioids were formally assessed on a regular basis. Furthermore, of those patients who did have pain or adverse effects monitored the frequency of observations was inadequate.

- In seven of the patients who received excessive doses of opioids there was lack of knowledge regarding acute pain management and inadequate clinical review of the escalating analgesic requirements. It was of particular note that in all of these cases, junior trainee medical staff were responsible for the prescribing of analgesia and no attempt was made to seek expert advice either from consultants in haemoglobinopathies or acute pain management.

Recommendations

- Healthcare professionals should work in partnership with patients with sickle cell disease to develop individualised pain management strategies which should include patient education. (Primary and Secondary Care Trusts)

- A multidisciplinary and multi-agency approach is needed in the ongoing pain management of patients with sickle cell disease – essentially this takes place outside hospitals for the majority of patients. (Primary and Secondary Care Trusts)

- Those patients with sickle cell disease and drug dependency need special attention because of the episodic nature of the pain and the consequent requirement for opioids which can exacerbate their dependency problems. (Primary and Secondary Care Trusts)

- Regular assessment of acute pain, sedation and respiratory rate should be undertaken and recorded for all patients admitted with sickle cell disease. The frequency of these observations should reflect the degree of pain and dose of opioids administered, to allow recognition of opioid overdose. The development of "track & trigger" systems would greatly enhance better pain control and patient safety. (Clinical Directors)

- Expert assistance from senior doctors with experience in the management of sickle cell pain should be sought at an early stage for patients whose pain is not controlled using standard methods. (Clinical Directors)

- Training for medical and nursing staff that care for patients with sickle cell disease in the management of both ongoing and acute pain needs to improve. This should include in-service training and specific tailor made courses for sickle cell pain management with regular updates. (Primary and Secondary Care Trusts)

References

1. Shapiro BS. *Pain in sickle cell disease*. IASP 1999, issue 10, article 9. http://www.nda.ox.ac.uk/wfsa/html/u10/u1009_01.htm

2. Biedrzycki O, Bevan D, Lucas SB. *Fatal fentanyl patch overdose in sickle cell patient*. American Journal of Forensic Medicine and Pathology. 2008 (in press).

3. McQuay M. *Consensus on outcome measures for chronic pain trials*. Pain 2005;113:1-2.

4. Rees DC, Olujohungbe AD, Parker NE *et al. Guidelines for the management of the acute painful crisis in sickle cell disease*. British Journal of Haematology 2003;120:744-52.

5. National Institute for Health and Clinical Excellence. *Acutely ill patients in hospital: Recognition of and response to acute illness in adults in hospital*. NICE clinical guideline 50. London, 2007. *http://www.nice.org.uk/nicemedia/pdf/ CG50FullGuidance.pdf*

6. ANZCA Acute Pain Management: Scientific Evidence 2nd Edition, section 4. 2005. *http://www.anzca.edu.au/resources/books-and-publications/acutepain.pdf*

6 – Final clinical management

Introduction

This chapter describes the final clinical management of the patients in the study. Most of the deaths were in hospital, following days or weeks of care and investigation, and will be referred to as final clinical episodes. A substantial proportion (14/55) of patients died in the community, with the patient being found dead at home or being declared dead in the emergency department. Of increasing interest in the literature, as a result of increasing survival, is sickle cell lung disease and its association with sudden death. A recent forensic pathology report [1] found that nearly three-quarters of sudden death patients with sickle cell disease had lung disease, including thromboembolism, oedema, pulmonary hypertension and microvascular occlusive thrombi.

Complications of sickle cell disease

A review of the casenotes showed that 17 of 41 patients who died in hospital experienced specific sickle-related complications in their final episode. The 17 patients, both adults and children, experienced 19 complications in total.

Stroke

This was the commonest complication and led to death in nine patients. All the formally diagnosed cases in adults were haemorrhagic rather than ischaemic (though some others may have been; it was not possible to determine). Whilst stroke in children with sickle cell disease is predominantly thrombotic occlusion, usually in adults it is haemorrhagic, resulting from sickle related damage to the cerebral vasculature [2]. There are no guidelines for prevention of stroke in adult sickle patients at present, as it is less tractable, but there are for children [3].

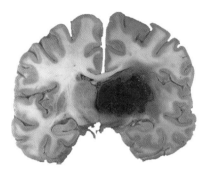

Figure 11. Intracerebral haemorrhage

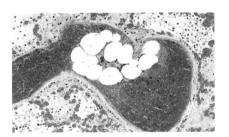

Figure 12. Fat embolism causing acute chest syndrome

Acute chest syndrome

Acute chest syndrome is a complication of sickle cell disease with a number of possible causes, including infection and fat embolism; it causes intra-pulmonary sickling and infarction. It commonly presents following a painful bone crisis. It is an important cause of mortality in patients with sickle cell disease and careful management is needed to reduce morbidity and mortality. The diagnosis may be missed and patients with sickle cell disease presenting with chest symptoms and signs need specific review with the possibility of acute chest syndrome in mind. Centres managing such patients should have clear protocols and guidelines for management and should have access to specialist advice. Exchange transfusion may be necessary in some cases.

There were two cases in which acute chest syndrome was listed as the primary cause of death, and three more where it was a likely contributor or part of multi-organ failure. Two further cases listed pneumonia as the cause of death. In addition, three cases had pulmonary hypertension or chronic lung disease listed as contributory causes of death.

There were no documented cases of acute chest syndrome causing death in children documented in this study, although this is a recognised cause of death in children [4].

Recommendation

- Acute chest syndrome is a major cause of morbidity and mortality in patients with sickle cell disease. Management of patients with this complication should be according to local protocols and early advice from specialists is essential. (Primary and Secondary Care Trusts)

Pulmonary embolism & hypertension

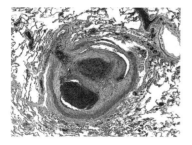

Figure 13. Chronic pulmonary vascular disease

Two patients died of massive pulmonary embolism, in both cases diagnosed at autopsy. There is no known association between sickle cell disease and deep vein thrombosis and/or pulmonary thromboembolism. Two patients were recorded to have pulmonary hypertension, and died of acute chest syndrome or multi-organ failure.

The advisors commented that diagnosing pulmonary embolism in sickle cell disease patients may be difficult, especially with regard to the chronic progressive lung disease that results from gradual thickening of the pulmonary arterial circulation. Both of these patients presented to hospital acutely ill and died within a day. The British Committee for Standards in Haematology (BCSH) guidelines (2003) [5] note that patients with sickle cell disease, confined to bed for more than 16 hours per day, should receive prophylactic anticoagulation.

Although pulmonary hypertension is being increasingly recognised in sickle cell disease patients [6, 7] it requires autopsy examination and extensive histopathology to fully determine the clinical pathology and the contribution of pulmonary hypertension to death.

Recommendation

- Chronic sickle chest disease is an expanding, complicated area and requires more careful correlation of pre-mortem clinical, physiological and imaging data with autopsy pathology. (Clinicians and Pathologists)

Sepsis

There were seven documented cases of infection (pneumonia n = 2, septicaemia n = 4 and bacterial peritonitis associated with cirrhosis n =1). Only two had organisms identified – both streptococcal infection, on blood culture (one stated to be *Streptococcal pneumoniae*). Pneumococcal infection is known to be associated with sickle cell disease. As far as could be determined from the records of the cases in the study, these specific infections were very acute. Outside the study, the pathology advisors had also seen community-acquired cases of pneumococcal sepsis presenting as rapidly progressive and fatal septic shock. This emphasises the importance of consideration of prophylactic penicillin and pneumococcal vaccination in sickle cell disease patients.

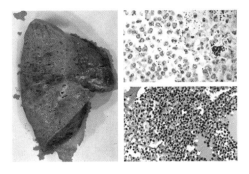

Figure 14. Streptococcus pneumoniae

Iron overload and cardiac death

Patients with transfusion-dependent beta thalassaemia major and intermedia and sickle cell disease can become severely iron overloaded if iron chelation therapy is either inadequate or not complied with. Iron overload can result in significant liver and cardiac damage, with the latter being the major cause of premature death in young adults with thalassaemia major. Avoidance of early death as well as long term complications due to iron overload requires close scrutiny by clinicians experienced in the management of haemoglobinopathies.

CASE STUDY 10

A young person with ß-thalassaemia major suffered a cardiac arrest in the community and could not be resuscitated. They were on desferral chelation therapy. Four months before death, for the first time, palpitations were noted when walking rapidly.

Palpitations may be an early sign of impending cardiac death in such patients and need attention from experienced clinicians. Although the ongoing care in this case appeared satisfactory, there was no record that this new symptom was investigated further.

Recommendation

- Patients with transfusion-dependent beta thalassaemia major need regular review at a specialist centre to ensure adequate assessment and management of iron overload. (Primary Care Trusts)

Renal failure

People with sickle cell disease are known to be at risk of renal failure. This may be due to damage to the renal glomerulus by the sickling process, infection or the use of nonsteroidal anti-inflammatory drugs. This has been a recognised problem for many years and is the subject of ongoing research [8, 9]. It is essential that all people with sickle cell disease should have their renal function monitored, including urinalysis for proteinuria and blood. Whilst no one dying in hospital was recorded as having renal complications of sickle cell disease as a cause of death, one case of chronic renal failure died at home and in another case renal failure was potentially overlooked.

CASE STUDY 11

A middle-aged patient with homozygous sickle cell anaemia was admitted for the management of medical problems including chronic renal failure. There was clear evidence of high-quality care and the patient was given a choice as to what should be done next. The patient chose not to have further investigations and intervention. There was a well-planned discharge into the community and the relevant team kept in contact, giving the patient the opportunity to change their mind. The patient subsequently died from renal failure.

While this was inevitably sad for the family, the terminal stage of life was clearly well managed.

And an example of poor care:

CASE STUDY 12

A young patient was admitted with increasing breathlessness for some weeks. As well as anaemia, there was a high urea of 27 mmol/L. The comment in the notes suggested that the serum creatinine should be measured before a decision was made whether there was renal failure. There was no evidence that this significant result was ever followed up.

Subsequently, the breathlessness was diagnosed as acute chest syndrome. Review by a chest physician doubted this, and suggested fluid overload. Again there was no follow-up of the renal function. A little later, the patient had a cardiac arrest, and the blood gas sample potassium result led to a diagnosis of 'hyperkalaemic cardiac arrest'.

The advisors' view was that after this unexpected death, there was a review of the case but no one appeared to have noted that initial high blood urea result. It was evident that this patient had had renal failure on admission which was not re-considered. The focus appeared to have been on the chest problems and adequate attention was not paid to the complete picture.

Recommendations

- New national standards for the management of sickle cell disease are soon to be issued and it is to be hoped that these will include regular review of renal function. (Department of Health)

- In all haemoglobinopathy patients who are acutely ill there should be a check to ensure that the kidneys are functioning properly. Acute illnesses may bring to light other problems such as renal tubular acidosis and all physicians caring for this group of patients must be aware of this. (Clinical Directors)

When sickle is not the main problem

People with sickle cell disease can, and do, develop other problems. There are some specific problems such as cholecystitis and septicaemia due to hyposplenism. In addition, a person with sickle cell disease can develop other medical problems seen in any individual. Many people with sickle cell disease complain that doctors tend to focus on the sickle cell disease alone and do not to listen to other problems. There was evidence to support this view within the cases reviewed. In addition, patients' notes were sometimes labelled in a way which might be described as prejudicial to their future care.

There was a clear example of a failure to look beyond sickle cell disease in other medical cases. In one patient with HIV, HbSC appears to have stopped the clinicians thinking beyond the patient's sickle cell disease.

Surgery and peri-operative care

Of the 41 patients who died in hospital, nine underwent surgical procedures in their final clinical episode. For the nine patients who underwent surgery, it was agreed by the advisors that the surgeon and anaesthetist had sufficient seniority and experience in four cases. In the remaining five cases, there was insufficient information. Therefore, there were no cases in which the advisors believed the surgeon and anaesthetist were not sufficiently experienced.

A further question considered by the advisors addressed peri-operative complications. Seven of the nine patients operated on, including both patients with sickle cell disease and thalassaemia, were considered to have had peri-operative complications.

More importantly, the advisors believed that in four of these cases, the complications could have been avoided. These avoidable complications were respectively, worsening liver failure and ascites, a massive cerebral infarct, a massive bleed and post-operative sepsis. The advisors commented that earlier recognition and intervention would have been possible and potentially prevented the complication. In the case of cerebral infarct, it was believed that blood transfusion may have prevented this problem.

Case study 14 highlights the need to look carefully at what is happening and not blame the problem solely on the sickle cell disease.

CASE STUDY 13

A young adult patient was thought to have an acute sickle cell crisis, but with rather atypical features. There did not appear to be a good response to standard treatment and the clinicians later reconsidered the working diagnosis. Further investigations showed the patient was HIV positive, with end-stage disease, which fitted better with the clinical scenario.

The advisors commented that had it not been for the sickle cell disease, it is likely that the problem would have been recognised more promptly.

Recommendations

- All staff should be aware that people with sickle cell disease are subject to the diseases that other patients suffer from as well. If there is uncertainty as to whether the problem is sickle cell related, advice should be sought from an experienced clinician. (Primary and Secondary Care Trusts)

- Patients with sickle cell disease are often very skilled in knowing exactly how their crises develop and if they say that this problem '"is different" then the clinician should pay heed and seek further advice if appropriate. (Primary and Secondary Care Trusts)

CASE STUDY 14

A middle-aged patient was admitted for an elective cholecystectomy. The surgery was undertaken late in the afternoon, followed by admission to a high dependency unit. A blood transfusion was given on the day of operation and, in addition, there was a large pre-operative fluid load. As the night progressed, the patient's condition deteriorated. The principal physical signs were a rising pulse and falling blood pressure – indicative of post-operative bleeding. The patient suffered a cardiac arrest and could not be resuscitated. At post mortem it was found that the abdomen was full of blood, from a post-operative haemorrhage.

This death might have been prevented by ensuring that the local protocols were followed. There was a clear guideline for the peri-operative management of this patient but it was the advisors' view that it had been poorly implemented. Additionally, common problems (post-op bleeding) occur commonly, even in patients with sickle cell disease and this should have been considered.

Key Finding

- There were fewer surgical cases submitted than were anticipated. NCEPOD is also aware of the on-going study of pre-operative blood transfusion [10].

Pregnancy

In this study population, there were no deaths in pregnancy or following delivery among the sickle cell disease patients. The latest CEMACH report [11] on maternal mortality covers the period 2003-5, and also recorded no fatalities directly related to sickle cell disease. However, in the year after the study closed, a pregnant woman with HbSC was known to have died of pneumococcal septic shock. In addition to sepsis, another potential morbidity around the time of delivery is the chronic vascular lung disease causing acute heart failure.

Sickle cell disease and thalassaemia in children

Sickle cell disease and thalassaemia are inherited, life-long conditions. Children with such conditions may present with associated problems as early as 3-6 months of age. They may, of course, also present with other unrelated illnesses. It is vital that these children are either managed or reviewed by clinicians who are experienced in the management of haemoglobinopathies or, at the very least, that advice from such a professional is sought early on in a patient's management. In this study, there were six patients under the age of 16 years. In four of these six deaths, it appeared that a complication related to sickle cell disease was the primary, or at least a contributory, cause of death.

It is of note that there were three community deaths in children with sickle cell disease; one due to pneumococcal sepsis, one due to stroke and one unknown cause of death.

As with adults, not all problems in children with sickle cell disease are related to their haemoglobinopathy status. However, in this study, sometimes the underlying diagnosis of sickle cell disease appeared to have confused or delayed the correct diagnosis, i.e. a lack of understanding of the possible complications of sickle cell disease. The following case study suggests this.

An adolescent with HbSS disease, regularly taking penicillin and folic acid, developed headache and vomiting. There was neck stiffness but no fever. The differential diagnosis was sickle crisis or meningitis. More antibiotics were given, but there was no record of a lumbar puncture being performed. The headache and vomiting persisted and a day later a CT scan was ordered. Although the initial report was normal, on review by the neurosurgical centre, it showed a subarachnoid haemorrhage. After transfer to this centre, a cerebral aneurysm was demonstrated and the patient had an exchange transfusion. There followed an intracerebral bleed, acute hydrocephalus and a shunt insertion. Two weeks later, a stent and coil embolisation of the aneurysm was performed but the patient deteriorated and died.

The advisors commented on the delay in considering an intracranial haemorrhage – a standard complication of sickle cell disease in children – and in obtaining a brain scan. They also considered why there appeared to be a delay in stenting the abnormal artery.

Advice and involvement from professionals with experience in the management of haemoglobinopathies in children should be sought early.

Pneumococcal prophylaxis and antibiotics

Sickle cell disease is associated with functional hyposplenism from an early age. As a consequence of this, children with sickle cell disease are at increased risk of infection, in particular from encapsulated organisms such as Streptococcus pneumoniae. Such infection is the major cause of mortality in children with sickle cell disease. Several studies have shown that penicillin prophylaxis and pneumococcal vaccination can reduce mortality from such infections and are, therefore, recommended from an early age. This problem has been recognised for over 25 years [12].

In this study, one child appeared to die from pneumococcal sepsis which is a preventable condition.

It was not clear from the review of the cases reported whether hospitals had clear protocols in place for antibiotic prophylaxis and vaccination in children with sickle cell disease.

Recommendations

- Guidelines and education about vaccination and antibiotic prophylaxis for children should be followed. (Primary Care Trusts)

- Early intervention is essential in children with sickle cell disease who become acutely unwell to reduce morbidity and morality. Expert advice should be sought. (Primary and Secondary Care Trusts)

Nursing care

In conducting the review, it was noted that overall nursing management of patients with sickle cell disease and thalassaemia was good. However, there was room for improvement in some significant areas, particularly relating to:

- The need to document all observations and actions accurately
- Reporting and acting on abnormal observations.
- Understanding the potential side effects of medications, especially opioids
- Importance of fluid balance and strict recording of input and output; and
- The need to maintain vigilance when patients are self-caring.

Observations

It is common for patients with sickle cell disease to be largely self-caring, especially when the severe acute episode has abated. However, assigning all patients with sickle cell disease who appear fairly well to the status of 'self-caring' can lead to a failure to recognise clinical problems. It should be evident that whilst a patient is an inpatient, in severe enough pain or state of ill health to warrant administration of opioids, other medication or treatment, they cannot be regarded as totally 'self-caring' and the ultimate responsibility for the patient management lies with the healthcare team. However involved in their own care the patient is, it is important that observations are routinely recorded and that any side effects or signs of deterioration are looked out for.

Table 7. Appropriate frequency of observations

Frequency of observations appropriate	Number of patients
Yes	27
No	6
Insufficient data	8
Total	**41**

The respiratory rate is a crucial observation in this patient group, but the advisors considered the frequency of observations to be inappropriate in six of the 41 patients who died in hospital (Table 7). In one case, evidence from the casenotes suggested that the nurses appeared to be unaware that one of the major side effects of using high doses of particular opioids is respiratory depression, cerebral irritation and possible convulsions. And in another case, even when the patient's conditions deteriorated (becoming very drowsy and non responsive), the nurses did not recognise whether this was a potential complication of sickle cell disease or a side effect of treatment.

CASE STUDY 16

A middle-aged patient with HbSC was admitted because of a painful crisis. Treatment was with pethidine at a dose of 50 mg every three hours. It was apparent from the notes that they were also taking long-term carbemazepine. While the reason for the carbamazepine was unclear, it is evident that a junior doctor in training doubled the dose of pethidine to 100 mg three-hourly. The patient had several doses at this level and was then found to be unresponsive.

The advisors reported that the reason for the patient to be taking carbamazepine was not apparent, and it raised the question as to whether or not the patient had epilepsy. If so, pethidine, a known epileptogenic drug, was considered to be an unwise choice. However, the situation might have been rescued by good nursing care since it is likely that the patient would have suffered a declining respiratory rate; unfortunately there was no evidence that this was monitored, despite the increase in the dose of pethidine.

Fluid balance

There appeared to be a lack of understanding of the importance of hydration in some patients with sickle cell disease. In just over half (21/41) of cases there was good and adequate management of fluid balance. However, in seven of the 41 cases there was poor management. In a further 13 cases there was insufficient data to be able to comment on the adequacy of fluid management.

In some instances there was evidence of poor fluid balance; that medical staff were unaware of. In one case doctors had requested, by writing in the patient's notes, that the nurses should ensure high fluid intake. However, there was a failure to monitor fluid intake and output and this contributed to the deterioration in the patient's condition.

In four cases the nursing staff failed to take action to ensure fluid balance and/or the documentation of input and output was poor.

One case provided a particularly clear demonstration of a lack of understanding of the importance of fluid balance management; in this case overhydration.

CASE STUDY 17

A patient with sickle cell disease suffered a cardiac arrest during an admission for the management of a painful crisis. The patient had been hypotensive two hours before the arrest, the cause of which was not adequately explained. Following the arrest there was cardio-pulmonary resuscitation, which went on for over two hours before death.

During the arrest procedure the patient was given three 500 ml infusions of a gelatin solution plus an unknown quantity of saline solution. Other intravenous fluids such as dextrose and sodium bicarbonate were also given. The patient's haemoglobin was measured towards the end of the arrest procedure and was 4.3 g/dL. On admission it had been 10.7 g/dL.

The advisors raised much speculation about the reasons for this drop in haemoglobin. No patient weight was indicated, but it is likely that a large part of the drop was due to dilution by intravenous fluids.

Key Findings

- Basic nursing observations, appropriately interpreted, are of critical importance to the management of people with sickle cell disease and were not always adhered to.

- Fluid balance was not well recorded in some patients and this contributed to deterioration in several patients clinical condition.

Recommendations

- All sickle cell disease patients should have a carefully maintained fluid balance chart for the duration of their admission. (Nurses)

- There is a need to ensure that any deterioration in vital signs is acted upon promptly. NCEPOD would urge those responsible for the continued development and education of staff to take note of these problems. (Clinical Directors)

Other Issues

Use of protocols

The use of clinical protocols has proven to be of enormous benefit in managing this patient group generally. In the few cases where they were used, it appeared that the multidisciplinary team had a better understanding of their role and responsibilities, plus an ability to recognise deviations from normal and the actions required.

The use of clinical protocols would enhance the overall care of this patient group nationally. It is recommended that a protocol be developed, widely advertised and made available to those caring for these patients. This should be aimed at clinicians working in specialist units as well as, perhaps more importantly, those working in non-specialist units and should be widely disseminated electronically.

Education

The lack of knowledge and understanding of sickle cell disease contributed in many instances to the failure of healthcare professionals to recognise the importance of observations, specific treatment modes and deviations from the normal.

Education about haemoglobinopathies, especially sickle cell disease and thalassaemia, should be a mandatory requirement for all nurses working in areas of moderate to high prevalence, notably major cities in the UK. Universities and hospitals providing training for medical students, nurses and other healthcare professionals should include information about sickle cell disease and thalassaemia in the educational curriculum of these professionals, at both the pre and post registration level.

In areas of low prevalence, opportunities should be provided for ad hoc training thus raising an awareness of these conditions. This could be provided through distance learning internet based packages or other learning methods.

Key Finding

- There were examples of failure to take action by both medical and nursing staff in the face of the deteriorating clinical condition of severely ill patients.

References

1. Graham JK, Mosunjac M, Hanzlick RL *et al. Sickle cell lung disease and sudden death: a retrospective/prospective study of 21 autopsy cases and literature review*. Am J Forensic Med Pathol. 2007;28(2):168-72.

2. Okpala I. *Practical Management of Haemoglobinopathies*. Blackwell publishing, 2004.

3. Stroke in childhood: Clinical guidelines for diagnosis, management and rehabilitation. Paediatric Stroke Working Party, Clinical Effectiveness and Evaluation Unit, Royal College of Physicians, 2004.

4. Platt OS, Brambilla DJ, Rosse WF *et al. Mortality in sickle cell disease. Life expectancy and risk factors for early death*. NEJM 1994;330(23):1639-44.

5. Rees DC, Olujohungbe AD, Parker NE *et al. Guidelines for the management of the acute painful crisis in sickle cell disease*. British Journal of Haematology 2003;120:744-52.

6. Haque AK, Gokhale S, Rampy BA *et al. Pulmonary hypertension in sickle cell hemoglobinopathy: a clinicopathologic study of 20 cases*. Hum Pathol 2002;33(10):1037-43.

7. Klings ES. *Pulmonary hypertension of sickle cell disease: more than just another lung disease*. Am J Hematol 2008;83(1):4-5.

8. Thompson J, Reid M, Hambleton I *et al. Albuminuria and Renal Function in Homozygous Sickle Cell Disease*. Archives of Internal Medicine 2007;167:701.

9. Powars DR, Elliott-Mills DD, Chan L *et al. Chronic renal failure in sickle cell disease: risk factors, clinical course, and mortality*. Annals of Internal Medicine 1991;115:614-20.

10. Transfusion Alternatives Pre-operatively in Sickle Cell Disease. *http://www.controlled-trials.com/cctspringview2/mrct/showTrial.html?mrid=273667&srch=*

11. Saving Mothers' Lives 2003-2005. Confidential Enquiry into Maternal and Child Health. 2007.

12. Landesman SH, Rao SP, Ahonkhai VI. *Infections in children with sickle cell anemia. Special reference to pneumococcal and salmonella infections*. The American Journal of Pediatric Hematology/Oncology 1982;4(4):407-18.

7 – Organisation of care

Introduction

Patients with sickle cell disease and beta thalassaemia major have a number of unique health problems and healthcare needs. They should be managed by clinicians with experience in managing haemoglobinopathies and have access to specialist review (on a regular basis).

Many of the cases in this study appeared not to have been managed by a specialist centre during their long-term follow up. Only 25 cases regularly attended specialist centres. Others were reviewed either by their GP or in a non specialist centre.

There were also cases that demonstrated high quality care where specialist advice was sought early in a patient's management.

With respect to outpatient care, this appeared to be quite variable, with some centres demonstrating regular review by experienced clinicians. In other cases however, it was difficult to identify adequate or appropriate follow-up for these often quite complex patients. It should be noted that this may have been because the relevant casenotes were not returned to NCEPOD.

It should also be noted that management of some haemoglobinopathy patients can be extremely difficult due to poor attendance and refusal to accept medical advice and treatment. Centres should have a local policy or guidance for management of patients who regularly fail to attend follow-up appointments.

Clinicians

Overall, 36/41 of patients were considered to have received combined care in their final episode. Due to the complex nature of the haemoglobinopathies, patients in hospital often require review by multiple specialties. Patients sometimes require referral to additional services, such as pain specialists or psychologists. There were examples of good multidisciplinary approaches and suitable referral in this study. However, there were also examples where a holistic multidisciplinary approach was considered to be lacking. This may be due to lack of availability of required services. The provision of services is described later in this chapter.

Despite the multidisciplinary nature of patient management, patients are still admitted under a named consultant. In this study, the most common admitting specialties were haematology (10) and general medicine (10). At the time of death, 13 patients were under the care of a consultant haematologist and six patients were under the care of an intensivist. The advisors considered there to be two patients who were admitted under an inappropriate specialty and not transferred to an appropriate clinician before the time of death. There were only six cases in which there was insufficient information to determine the admitting specialty and five cases where the clinician at the time of death was not documented.

There were eight patients whom the advisors considered to have had an inadequate frequency of reviews in their final episode.

Hospital and wards

Twenty seven patients were managed at a hospital with a haemoglobinopathy team. The advisors considered five patients to have been admitted to an initial hospital that was not suitable for managing their haemoglobinopathy. In four of these cases, the patient was not transferred to a more appropriate hospital. In three of these cases, it was believed that the unsuitability of the hospital may have influenced the outcome.

Patients with multiple co-morbidities, needing multidisciplinary care, pose problems as to the best place for them to be managed. In this study, the advisors considered that there was lack of clarity about where the patient should have been managed in five cases. This caused delay. In one case, a medical patient was managed on a surgical ward. In another, there was a considerable delay in recognising the severity of the complications and admitting the patient to the Intensive Care Unit.

There was one case (case study 18) that highlighted a specific difficulty; the grey area between paediatric and adult care.

An adolescent patient with thalassaemia and diabetes mellitus presented to the haemoglobinopathy unit at a paediatric hospital with a several day history of feeling weak and high temperature. On admission, blood pressure was unrecordable and only one respiratory rate was measured. The patient was eventually transferred to the paediatric intensive care unit and emergency bowel surgery performed. The patient died 14 days after presentation with multi-organ failure.

The advisors believed that an adult unit would have had better experience, equipment and medications for management of a post-paediatric thalassaemia patient.

Seeking advice

Previous NCEPOD studies have highlighted the need for consultant input into the management of acutely sick patients at an early stage [1]. This study again emphasised the need to have an appropriately experienced senior clinician involved at an early stage in order to avoid morbidity and mortality. People with sickle cell disease can develop a number of complications including cerebral vascular accidents, acute chest syndrome and renal failure. Staff caring for these patients must be aware of the possible complications of sickle cell disease and that these patients can deteriorate very rapidly. It is important to avoid being complacent; this is particularly true for those patients who are seen as 'regular attenders' since they too can, and do, develop some of these complications. There is a need for a holistic approach to these patients and this was often missing. Sadly, some patients seem to have been pre-labelled as being "problem patients". For example, one patient's notes were labelled to show that they were violent and abusive. This may have been the case in the past, but there was no evidence that this was so during the final admission and it was unfortunate that this type of labelling may have influenced the approach to their problems.

In this study, there were four cases in which it was judged by the advisors that advice was not sought from external experts when required. There were a further five cases where it was believed that junior doctors did not seek advice from senior doctors when it was necessary to do so. Examples of the failure to seek advice are presented in case studies 19 and 20.

CASE STUDY 19

A middle-aged patient presented with clinical evidence of a cerebral vascular accident and was shown to have had an acute haemorrhagic stroke. This was managed both surgically and medically, but there was no evidence to suggest any input by a haematologist. The anaemia (Hb 6.6 g/dL) was not treated and there was no evidence of the patient having been exchanged transfused. Some days later there was a further stroke and the patient died.

The advisors believed that this might have been avoided if a transfusion had taken place, and at the very least this matter should have been considered by a senior haematology consultant.

CASE STUDY 20

A Specialist Registrar made the decision to stop the warfarin in a young patient with a history of pulmonary embolism who was undergoing eye surgery for a cataract. There was no consideration given to starting heparin post operatively. The patient developed a post operative pulmonary embolus and died.

The advisors believed that there should have been a haematology consultant involved in the complicated decisions around the patient's anticoagulation therapy. There ought to have been a way around this problem of prophylaxis.

The clinicians completing the questionnaire were asked if, in their opinion, there were issues related to the training of the medical team and junior doctors in the management of haemoglobinopathies. Twelve clinicians commented on areas of concern. Two clinicians believed that the recognition of potentially life threatening sepsis in the community needed to be addressed. There was one case where a child was not taking penicillin in the community because of vomiting. There was also considered to be a lack of education – including amongst Emergency Department doctors – and awareness that not all crises involve pain. A poor understanding of fluid management, transfusion risks and failure to seek a specialist opinion were among the other points raised.

Hospital facilities

The 47 patients for whom there was a questionnaire completed were managed at 26 different hospital sites. The third section of the questionnaire asked details of the organisation of patient management within the hospital. For those sites with more than one included patient, the questionnaire returned closest to the middle of the study (end of December 2005) was used for the organisational analysis.

Twelve centres provided data on the number of sickle cell disease patients managed at the unit in the year April 2003 – March 2004. The number of sickle cell disease patients managed at each of the units varied from two to 600. Three hospitals managed 10 or less sickle cell disease patients. At the other end of the spectrum, seven hospitals managed 200 or more sickle cell disease patients.

There were 15 units that did not have data on the number of thalassaemia patients who were managed at the unit in the same year period. Of the eleven units for which data were available, six units managed fewer than 10 thalassaemia patients; three had only one thalassaemia patient.

Sixteen of the 26 units had a dedicated haemoglobinopathy team. In 13 of these units, there was a sickle cell disease and thalassaemia team. In the other three units, there was a sickle cell team only. All of these units had regular access to a haematologist. Thirteen units had regular access to a nurse practitioner, 10 to a pain specialist, five to an anaesthetic specialist and eight to a psychologist. The pain specialist was a doctor in six units; four of which also had a nurse pain specialist.

Protocols and guidelines

In the cases reviewed in this study there was evidence of some excellent protocols being available for the management of these patients. However, these protocols were not always followed.

Many centres had detailed and comprehensive protocols, although some were too brief for the complicated scenarios seen. There were good examples of protocols, in particular the 'patient passport' to help guide Emergency Department doctors in a patient's management.

Table 8. Available guidelines

Guidelines	Number available
Pain	19
Pregnancy	11
Sequestration crisis	13
Priapism	13
Acute anaemia	14
Acute chest syndrome	17
Chronic renal failure	6
General anaesthesia	13
Iron-chelation therapy	10
Blood transfusion	13

Only four of the 26 hospitals had a care pathway for haemoglobinopathy patients. The availability of guidelines for specific management issues was more promising. Of the 26 sites at which patients were managed, the most common guidelines were in the management of pain. Nineteen units had guidelines for the management of pain. The availability of a range of guidelines is illustrated in Table 8. Three units reported having no guidelines.

The management of paediatric patients differs from that of adult patients. However, only 10 of the sites documented having separate guidelines for the management of paediatric and adult patients. Two of the eight sites that did not have separate guidelines were paediatric hospitals and so adult guidelines would not be necessary.

Less than a third (8/26) of sites had agreed policies with other hospitals for the transfer of sickle cell disease patients. This may be because the hospital at which the patient was being managed was a specialist haemoglobinopathy hospital, but this does not negate the need for policies for transfer of patients to the unit or to another unit for a different service.

Recommendations

- Patients with sickle cell disease or beta thalassaemia major should be managed by, or have access to, clinicians with experience of haemoglobinopathy management. (Primary and Secondary Care Trusts)

- All patients with sickle cell disease or beta thalassaemia major should be reviewed at least annually at a specialist centre. (Primary Care Trusts)

- All haemoglobinopathy patients should have a named specialist, ideally a haematologist, responsible for their care. The haematologist must have an appropriate level of expertise to care for the patient or should make links with appropriate experts. (Primary and Secondary Care Trusts)

- Healthcare centres responsible for the management of patients with haemoglobinopathies should have access to protocols/guidelines from their regional specialist centre. (Primary and Secondary Care Trusts)

Reference

1. An acute problem? National confidential Enquiry into Patient Outcome and Death, 2005
   www.ncepod.org.uk

8 – Death certification and autopsies

Introduction

The Royal College of Pathologists issued a set of autopsy guidelines for best practice in 2005 (now consolidated in a single document RCPath Guidelines for Autopsy Practice, 2008) [1, 2]. These include a protocol for examining patients with sickle cell disease and cover most of the clinico-pathological scenarios encountered. The correct formulation of the cause of death at autopsy is also indicated with specific examples.

Death certification by doctors in England and Wales has been reviewed previously and has highlighted the deficiencies in the process in terms of accuracy and relevance [3]. Recently, the Department of Health in England has consulted on a major review of death certification with proposals to introduce medical examiners nationally, to ensure standardised scrutiny of causes of death and consideration of reporting cases to coroners [4].

The General Register Office issued revised guidance on how to complete medical certificates of cause of death in 2005 [5] and in 2007 the Chief Medical Officer in England wrote to all doctors exhorting them to take death certification more seriously, giving more accurate causes of death (and with particular reference to healthcare associated infections) [6].

Death certification

The cause of death could be determined from the notes or the clinician questionnaire in the majority of cases. However, there were 12 cases in which the cause of death was not stated in either the casenotes or the questionnaire. In the remaining 43 cases, the advisors agreed with the documented cause of death in 22 cases. However, there were 18 cases in which the cause of death was considered to be incorrect based on the casenote evidence. There were a further three cases in which the advisors could not make an assessment from the available data (Figure 15).

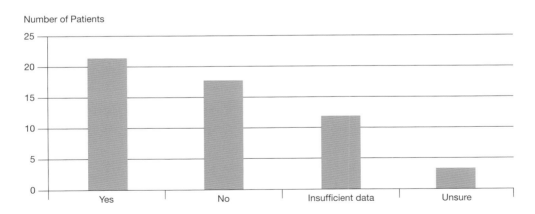

Number of Patients

Figure 15. Correct cause of death: Advisors' opinion

Reasons for incorrect death certification documentation included failure to include sickle cell disease on the death certificate, incorrect ordering of contributing factors (i.e. confusing parts 1 and 2 in the formulation) and a failure to include operation details.

In four cases, sickle cell disease was not mentioned anywhere in the certified cause of death and yet was the primary disease causing death. In one case, the pathologist, after autopsy, gave the cause of death as:
1a.   Decompensated cor pulmonale.

In a second case, a patient with subarachnoid haemorrhage, it was agreed that the evidence showed that sickle cell disease was the cause of the arteriopathy leading to haemorrhage, yet sickle cell disease was not mentioned in the death certificate.

Conversely, in two cases sickle cell disease was listed under part 1, whilst the advisors thought that sickle cell disease was only contributory and should have been listed under part 2. For example, a baby who died of complications of prematurity in which the sickle cell disease was of minor significance in the problems.

In two cases, there was a misunderstanding of the correct way to complete a death certificate.
For example, one certificate was completed thus:
1a   Sickle cell disease
1b   Severe haemolytic anaemia
1c   Cardiorespiratory arrest
This was completely the wrong way round.

Autopsies

Patients who die with sickle cell-related conditions and an unclear cause of death do not always have an autopsy. On review of the available casenotes, it was found that 21 of the 55 patients in the study had an autopsy. Of these, 20 were coronial autopsies and one was a hospital autopsy. A further two patients were referred to the coroner, but no autopsy was performed.

In five cases, where there was no evidence of an autopsy being performed, the advisors believed that an autopsy was necessary to determine the cause of death.

Clinicians sometimes requested a coronial autopsy when a hospital autopsy might have been better. Fifteen autopsy reports were returned to NCEPOD and the review of these reports forms the basis of the remainder of this chapter.

However, the overall standard of autopsy reports was poor. Commonly, they did not address the clinical problems documented in life and in several cases it appears that the knowledge of the history of sickle cell disease biased the issuing of a cause of death which did not always correlate with the clinical scenario, i.e. deaths in sickle patients are not by definition always caused by that disease. There were several examples of excellent and thorough autopsies, with detailed reports. A case study is detailed below.

CASE STUDY 21

A young adult suffered a pulmonary embolism secondary to a deep vein thrombosis. Full histology was undertaken which documented the bone necrosis present and the changes of pulmonary hypertension, both significant problems clinically. In addition, toxicology was undertaken as the death occurred soon after the administration of diamorphine. A therapeutic level of diamorphine, in keeping with the administered dose, was confirmed.

The advisors reported that the clinico-pathological correlation went on to describe that deep vein thromboses and pulmonary embolisation were not common problems in sickle cell disease patients.

Of the 13 adult autopsies for which reports were available, the advisors, in the context of the available clinical information:

Agreed with the autopsy diagnosis 4
Disagreed with the autopsy diagnosis 3
Found the autopsy diagnosis most probably
not correct or simply unknown 6

This proportion of unhelpful autopsies is marked. Clinicians and families are not served by such reports.

There were two cases of particular note. Both were coronial autopsies undertaken for unexplained deaths at home. Both patients had a history of drug dependency and drug abuse. In neither case was the brain examined, nor were toxicology or histology undertaken.

CASE STUDY 22

In this adult patient with a history of drug abuse, the main findings described were cardiomegaly and hepatomegaly, with the cause of death given as:

1a. Cardiomegaly

1b. Sickle cell disease

2.   Hepatomegaly

The advisors considered that the terms cardiomegaly and hepatomegaly describe enlarged organs but give no indication of the diseases causing the enlargement. Intracerebral haemorrhage is a common cause of death in sickle cell disease, but could not be excluded by this autopsy because the brain was not examined. Because of the known history of drug abuse, the possibility of drug overdose should have been considered and excluded, but no toxicology was taken.

CASE STUDY 23

The body showed significant decomposition with inhaled gastric contents in the bronchi and gaseous abdominal distension. The cause of death was given as:

1a   Inhalation of stomach contents

1b   Intestinal obstruction

1c   Intestinal adhesions

The advisors commented that inhalation of gastric contents can occur in the terminal stages of both intracerebral haemorrhage and drug overdose, neither of which was excluded by this autopsy. Furthermore, the evidence for intestinal obstruction was poorly described, with the advisors' opinion being that post mortem decomposition was the most likely cause of the gaseous dilation.

The failure to perform histology in several of the cases was of concern, with the likelihood that incorrect causes of death may have been given. Histology was only taken in five of the 15 autopsies reviewed in the study; two further cases indicate how histological examination might have helped, particularly in establishing a diagnosis of acute chest syndrome, which the advisors suspect was underdiagnosed in the study cohort.

CASE STUDY 24

A middle-aged patient was admitted with painful sickle cell crisis and was being treated as per the hospital protocol. All observations were normal. The patient suffered an unexpected cardiac arrest. On morphological appearances of the kidney alone, with no confirmatory histology, the pathologist gave the cause of death as renal failure due to renal papillary necrosis. However, at autopsy the bladder was full of urine, and throughout the admission the renal function was measured as normal.

It was the opinion of the advisors that the patient could not have died from renal failure secondary to papillary necrosis with investigations showing normal electrolytes and renal function only a few hours prior to death. The real cause of death may have been the acute chest syndrome.

CASE STUDY 25

A young person was admitted to the ICU with a history of abdominal pain and severe metabolic acidosis. A liver biopsy taken in life showed liver necrosis but did not identify the cause. Due to the patient's condition, further invasive procedures could not be undertaken, although sickle cell trait was identified on a blood test. At autopsy, areas of infarction were seen in the brain, kidney, liver and spleen. Despite the liver biopsy not being diagnostic, no post mortem histology was undertaken and the multiple infarctions were attributed to sickle cell trait.

The advisors reported that sickle cell trait is a rare cause of infarction, particularly in the presence of severe hypoxia; but the presenting history did not suggest that sickle cell trait was relevant. As a result, the case was excluded from the main study analysis, but it raises an important point. There are many other causes of multiple organ infarction, such as vasculitis, which might have been identified had histology been undertaken.

Conversely, a case already described (Case study 2) indicates the problems that sickle cell trait can present for clinico-pathological interpretation at autopsy.

The value of histology was shown in a contrasting case where the patient was admitted with abdominal pain with surgical excision of a necrotic caecum. The histology of the caecum did not identify the cause of the necrosis. Post operatively the patient developed neurological problems and scans revealed infarcts in the brain, kidney, liver and spleen. These were confirmed at autopsy. Post mortem histology was taken and was crucial in determining that the infarcts were due to mucormycosis, which was secondary to diabetes due to haemosiderosis caused by transfusion for thalassaemia.

In another case, histology was important in identifying the correct cause of death of a young patient with multiple admissions for acute chest syndrome. On the last admission the patient did not respond as expected to the exchange transfusion. The case was a coronial autopsy and histology was undertaken which showed that the patient suffered from septic shock in addition to the acute chest syndrome for which he was admitted. This explained why the patient did not respond as expected to the treatment given.

Specialist autopsy pathology

Since 1989, NCEPOD reports have recommended improvements in the care with which pathologists undertake autopsies in complex clinical cases, in the accuracy to which coronial autopsies are performed and in a more holistic approach to formulating causes of death. Review of the admittedly small number of cases within this study shows that in the context of the complex haemoglobinopathy diseases, pathologists and clinicians have problems in correctly correlating the sequence of events that led to death. Few pathologists have any significant practical experience of sickle cell disease and its interpretation, though there are Royal College of Pathologists guidelines to aid this process. Non-sickle-specialist clinicians are in a similar position. Moreover, owing to the current coronial system, coroners are not necessarily interested in the precise and quantifiable role of sickle cell disease in a death. As long as the sequence leading to death is not 'unnatural', then the routine Coroner's Act (1988) section 19 autopsy fulfils its fundamental purpose if it (only) provides information that renders an inquest unnecessary [7].

Key Finding

- Deaths in sickle cell disease patients were not well evaluated and depicted.

Recommendations

- Cause of death in sickle cell disease patients must be better evaluated, whether by clinicians reviewing the records and writing a death certificate or by pathologists performing an autopsy. Clinico-pathological correlation is critical in this complex disease. (Clinicians and Pathologists)

References

1. Guidelines for Autopsy Practice, Royal College of Pathologists, 2008 www.rcpath.org.uk

2. Guidelines on Autopsy Practice – best practice scenarios. Royal College of Pathologists, scenario 2, 2005.

3. Clarke A, Gladwin E. Improving the health of the living? An investigation into death certification and coronial services and some suggestions for change. Report from the London School of Hygiene and Tropical Medicine, to The Fundamental Review of Death Certification and the Coroner Services in England, Wales and Northern Ireland. Jan 2003.

4. Consultation on Improving the Process of Death Certification, Department of Health consultation document, Department of Health, 2007. http://www.dh.gov.uk/en/Consultations/Closedconsultations/DH_076971

5. www.gro.gov.uk/medcert

6. CMO letter, August 2007.

7. The Coroner's Autopsy: Do we deserve better? National Confidential Enquiry into Patient Outcome and Death. 2006. www.ncepod.org.uk

9 – Summary and comment

This review of deaths from haemoglobinopathy over two years was proposed to provide insights into remediable factors that can improve the care of these patients and to indicate the current clinico-pathological scenarios that result in death. The documentary information (on clinical and pathological matters) was not complete for all the cases that were reported and therefore the study size is small. Nonetheless, a notable finding was the high proportion of cases (nearly half) where, using this method of clinical review, the actual cause of death was debatable or unknown. If this small series is representative, it amounts to a wake-up call to the haemoglobinopathy clinical community: less is known about the severe complications of sickle cell disease that lead to death in individual patients than was previously thought. It prompts the conclusion that a national database of haemoglobinopathy patients is needed and a rigorous systematic audit of their deaths that incorporates as much objective information (including focussed specialist autopsies) as possible. Only by this means will haemoglobinopathy mortality be better understood and more knowledge available on how to reduce it.

Monitoring patients

As in previous studies, NCEPOD has highlighted examples where patients who were acutely ill were not offered support from sufficiently experienced medical staff. NCEPOD firmly believe that there is a need to monitor patients on opioids more carefully. Nurses and doctors both need to be more familiar with what needs to be done if patients' vital signs, including the respiratory rate, become abnormal. These simple measures might well have avoided some of these deaths.

Clinical networks

There is a move towards establishing clinical networks. While these will offer some benefit, there will still be a problem for people with sickle cell disease who present to remote units lacking experience in managing the complications of this condition. It is important that all haematologists who have a responsibility for managing people with sickle cell disease or thalassaemia have access to appropriately qualified colleagues who can offer support, where required. It may not be possible to easily transfer an acutely sick individual, especially if they are already experiencing considerable pain.

There is a need for holistic care for people with haemoglobinopathies. Most will need long term medications with all of the difficulties that this can bring in terms of compliance. Specialist centres, with support from nurses, psychologists and other healthcare professionals are necessary to ensure optimum care and compliance.

It is essential that centres offering support for acutely ill patients with haemoglobinopathies should have consultants with appropriate experience available at all times and that these consultants ensure that local guidelines and national standards, when developed, are adhered to. This will need auditing.

Development of national guidelines

As part of the study, NCEPOD was supplied with many local guidelines. It is also understood that there is now a nationally accepted management protocol for people with thalassaemia but that the equivalent overarching document for people with sickle cell disease is still in preparation. NCEPOD believes that the Sickle Cell Society has sponsored the preparation of an appropriate national guideline; it is hoped that this guideline will be produced in the near future and that it will be implemented and audited appropriately.

Given the clinical problems that arise in people with sickle cell disease, it is hoped that national guidelines will become available for:
- The management of acute chest syndrome
- The appropriate management of acute infections
- The acutely deteriorating sickle cell patient
- Deteriorating renal function
- The use of opioid drugs, and how to avoid dependency and to manage it.

National database of haemoglobinopathy patients

Within the body of the report a number of references have been made to the fact that there is no national database of those affected by sickle cell disease; it is understood that there is a thalassaemia database but that there have been problems in maintaining it. There is now a policy to implement a national database for haemoglobinopathies and NCEPOD would strongly support this.

Such a database will bring benefit to the patients because it will make it possible to understand more about the problems that arise within the affected communities. For example, during the study it was discovered that two of the deaths in people with sickle cell anaemia appeared to be due to coexistent systemic lupus erythematosus. One of the team undertaking this study believed that this problem may be more prevalent in the sickle cell community than expected. However, because there is no database, it is impossible to know the exact denominator and one cannot, therefore, be certain as to whether this observation is an artefact or a genuine and potentially important difference which requires further research. A database would also allow better comparison with the outcomes achieved within the setting of the NHS and with patients in other major centres, such as those in Jamaica or the United States of America.

Such information may in turn lead to improvements in the care of people affected by sickle cell disease in particular. Differences in management strategies, such as the use of non-steroidal anti-inflammatory drugs instead of opioid analgesics may, over time, have a significant impact on, for example, the incidence of renal failure within the community. In the absence of a national database it will be difficult to prove such possibilities, to the disadvantage of all concerned.

Pain control

This study has demonstrated that pain and its management presents a major problem for patients with sickle cell disease. The episodic nature of the disease is notable in the requirements for opioid analgesics potentially in high doses. The complexity of this pain poses significant challenges for those who have sickle cell disease, as well as the healthcare professionals who care for them. In this study there were examples of poor multidisciplinary team working in both ongoing pain and acute pain management.

For the tiny minority of patients who develop drug dependency there is a need to ensure that appropriate services are made available in order to help them deal with this problem.

A recurring theme from this study was the excessive doses of opioid analgesics in patients with painful crises. There appeared to be a lack of understanding of the adverse effects of these drugs by doctors and nurses. In addition, assessment of pain, sedation and respiratory rate was infrequently performed.

For the situation to be improved there needs to be better education and training in pain control management for healthcare professions who care for patients with sickle cell disease. Experts in acute and chronic pain control should be major contributors in the care of these patients. Trusts need to develop local written protocols for the management of painful episodes based on national guidelines and local facilities. These should include regular clinical review to determine the efficacy of the pain therapy and avoid overdose. The use of "track & trigger" systems would greatly enhance better pain control and patient safety. Furthermore, patients need to be encouraged to be active participants in the management of their pain. This will require enhanced patient education to improve understanding so that they can accept greater responsibility for their pain control. There is a case for doing more clinical research into pain management techniques for this group of patients.

Autopsy evaluation and causes of death

The quality of autopsies was poor; this problem has been investigated previously [1]. In nine of the 13 adult cases with an autopsy report to review, the advisors either disagreed with the interpretation, or found the autopsy unintepretable. It is essential that autopsies should be properly conducted, by experienced pathologists availing themselves of full investigations, so that an understanding of the problems leading to death can be properly delineated.

Some problems, such as acute chest syndrome, are complex and may be due to a range of underlying problems. Histological examination is important; care should be taken in interpreting findings since post mortem sickling may otherwise be misinterpreted as having contributed to death. The evaluation of the chronic lung pathologies associated with sickle cell disease is even more complicated. Properly conducted autopsies may still have a lot to contribute to a better understanding of issues such as stroke and lung disease.

Recommendation

- A national database of patients with haemoglobinopathies should be developed and maintained, to include standardised information on death, for regular audit purposes. (Department of Health)

Reference

1. The Coroner's Autopsy: Do we deserve better? National Confidential Enquiry into Patient Outcome and Death. 2006
   www.ncepod.org.uk

Appendices

Appendix A

Glossary

ACS	Acute chest syndrome
BCSH	British Committee for Standards in Haematology
CEMACH	Confidential Enquiry into Maternal and Child Health
CT	Computed tomography
GP	General Practitioner
Hb	Haemoglobin
HbAS	Sickle cell trait
HbSC	Sickle haemoglobin C
HbSD	Sickle haemoglobin D
HbSS	Sickle cell anaemia
HbS ß-Thal	Sickle ß-thalassaemia
HIV	Human immunodeficiency virus
ICD-10	International Classification of Diseases, 10th revision
ICU	Intensive care unit
IV	Intravenous
NCEPOD	National Confidential Enquiry into Patient Outcome and Death
NHS	National Health Service
NSAID	Non-steroidal anti-inflammatory drug
ONS	Office for National Statistics
RCPath	Royal College of Pathologists
SHO	Senior house officer
SLE	Systemic lupus erythematosus
TPR	Temperature, pulse and respiration
UK	United Kingdom
USA	United States of America
WHO	World Health Organisation

Appendix B

Participating trusts and specialist centres

Adur, Arun and Worthing Primary Care Trust
Aintree Hospitals NHS Trust
Airedale NHS Trust
Altnagelvin Hospitals Health & Social Services Trust
Amber Valley Primary Care Trust
Ashford & St Peter's Hospital NHS Trust
Aspen Healthcare
Barking, Havering and Redbridge Hospitals NHS Trust
Barnsley Hospital NHS Foundation Trust
Bart's and The London NHS Trust
Basildon & Thurrock University Hospitals NHS FoundationTrust
Bedford Hospital NHS Trust
Bedfordshire Heartlands Primary Care Trust
Belfast City Hospital Health & Social Services Trust
Birmingham Childrens Hospital NHS Trust
Blackpool, Fylde and Wyre Hospitals NHS Trust
Blackwater Valley and Hart Primary Care Trust
BMI Healthcare
Bolton Hospitals NHS Trust
Bradford Teaching Hospitals NHS Foundation Trust
Brighton and Sussex University Hospitals NHS Trust
Bromley Hospitals NHS Trust
Buckinghamshire Hospitals NHS Trust
BUPA
Burton Hospitals NHS Trust
Cambridge University Hospitals NHS Foundation Trust
Camden Primary Care Trust
Capio Health Care UK
Cardiothoracic Centre Liverpool NHS Trust (The)
Carmarthenshire NHS Trust
Causeway Health & Social Services Trust
Central Liverpool Primary Care Trust

Central Manchester & Manchester Children's
Ceredigion & Mid Wales NHS Trust
Chelsea & Westminster Healthcare NHS Trust
Chesterfield & North Derbyshire Royal Hospital NHS Trust
Chesterfield Primary Care Trust
Chiltern and South Bucks Primary Care Trust
Christie Hospital NHS Trust
City Hospitals Sunderland NHS Foundation Trust
Classic Hospitals
Conwy & Denbighshire NHS Trust
Countess of Chester Hospital NHS Foundation Trust
Covenant Healthcare Limted
Craigavon Area Hospital Group Trust
Cromwell Hospital
Dartford & Gravesham NHS Trust
Dartford, Gravesham & Swanley Primary Care Trust
Daventry & South Northants Primary Care Trust
Derby Hospitals NHS Foundation Trust
Doncaster and Bassetlaw Hospitals NHS Foundation Trust
Doncaster Central Primary Care Trust
Down Lisburn Health & Social Services Trust
Dudley Group of Hospitals NHS Trust
Durham Dales Primary Care Trust
Ealing Hospital NHS Trust
East & North Hertfordshire NHS Trust
East Cheshire NHS Trust
East Devon Primary Care Trust
East Elmbridge and Mid Surrey Primary Care Trust
East Hampshire Primary Care Trust
East Kent Hospitals NHS Trust
East Kent Medical Services
East Lancashire Hospitals NHS Trust
East Somerset NHS Trust
East Sussex Hospitals NHS Trust

Epsom and St Helier University Hospitals NHS Trust

Essex Rivers Healthcare NHS Trust

Fairfield Independent Hospital

Fareham & Gosport Primary Care Trust

Frimley Park Hospitals NHS Trust

George Eliot Hospital NHS Trust

Good Hope Hospital NHS Trust

Great Ormond Street Hospital for Children NHS Trust (The)

Gwent Healthcare NHS Trust

Hammersmith Hospitals NHS Trust

Haringey Teaching Primary Care Trust

Harlow Primary Care Trust

Harrogate and District NHS Foundation Trust

Harrow Primary Care Trust

HCA International

Health & Social Services, States of Guernsey

Heatherwood and Wexham Park Hospitals NHS Trust

Hereford Hospitals NHS Trust

Hertsmere Primary Care Trust

High Peak & Dales Primary Care Trust

Hillingdon Primary Care Trust

Hinchingbrooke Health Care NHS Trust

Homerton University Hospital NHS Foundation Trust

Hospital of St John and St Elizabeth

Hull and East Yorkshire Hospitals NHS Trust

Ipswich Hospital NHS Trust

Isle of Man Department of Health & Social Security

Isle of Wight Healthcare NHS Trust

James Paget Healthcare NHS Trust

Kennet and North Wiltshire Primary Care Trust

King Edward VII's Hospital Sister Agnes

King's College Hospital NHS Trust

King's Lynn & Wisbech Hospitals NHS Trust

Kingston Hospital NHS Trust

Kingston Primary Care Trust

Lancashire Teaching Hospitals NHS Foundation Trust

Leeds Teaching Hospitals NHS Trust (The)

Lewisham Hospital NHS Trust

London Clinic

Luton and Dunstable Hospital NHS Trust

Maidstone and Tunbridge Wells NHS Trust

Maidstone Weald Primary Care Trust

Mansfield District Primary Care Trust

Mater Hospital Belfast Health & Social Services Trust

Mayday Health Care NHS Trust

Medway NHS Trust

Mendip Primary Care Trust

Mid Cheshire Hospitals NHS Trust

Mid Devon Primary Care Trust

Mid Staffordshire General Hospitals NHS Trust

Mid Yorkshire Hospitals NHS Trust

Mid-Essex Hospital Services NHS Trust

Milton Keynes Primary Care Trust

Moorfields Eye Hospital NHS Foundation Trust

Morecambe Bay Hospitals NHS Trust

Mount Alvernia Hospital

Newcastle upon Tyne Hospitals NHS Trust

Newham Healthcare NHS Trust

Norfolk & Norwich University Hospital NHS Trust

North Bradford Primary Care Trust

North Cheshire Hospitals NHS Trust

North Cumbria Acute Hospitals NHS Trust

North Devon Primary Care Trust

North East Wales NHS Trust

North Eastern Derbyshire Primary Care Trust

North Glamorgan NHS Trust

North Hampshire Hospitals NHS Trust

North Middlesex University Hospital NHS Trust

North Norfolk Primary Care Trust

North Tees and Hartlepool NHS Trust
North West London Hospitals NHS Trust
Northampton General Hospital NHS Trust
Northern Devon Healthcare NHS Trust
Northern Lincolnshire & Goole Hospitals Trust
Nottingham City Hospital NHS Trust
Nottinghamshire Healthcare NHS Trust
Nuffield
Oxford Radcliffe Hospital NHS Trust
Papworth Hospital NHS Foundation Trust
Pembrokeshire & Derwen NHS Trust
Pennine Acute Hospitals NHS Trust (The)
Peterborough & Stamford Hospitals NHS FoundationTrust
Plymouth Hospitals NHS Trust
Poole Hospital NHS Trust
Portsmouth Hospitals NHS Trust
Powys Local Health Board
Preston Primary Care Trust
Princess Alexandra Hospital NHS Trust
Queen Elizabeth Hospital NHS Trust
Queen Mary's Sidcup NHS Trust
Queen Victoria Hospital NHS Foundation Trust
Reading Primary Care Trust
Robert Jones and Agnes Hunt Orthopaedic
& District Hospital
Rotherham General Hospitals NHS Trust
Royal Berkshire and Battle Hospitals NHS Trust
Royal Bournemouth and Christchurch Hospitals
NHS Trust
Royal Brompton and Harefield NHS Trust
Royal Cornwall Hospitals NHS Trust
Royal Devon and Exeter NHS Foundation Trust
Royal Free Hampstead NHS Trust
Royal Group of Hospitals & Dental Hospitals &
Maternity Hospitals
Royal Liverpool and Broadgreen University Hospitals
NHS Trust
Royal Liverpool Children's NHS Trust
Royal Marsden NHS Foundation Trust (The)

Royal National Orthopaedic Hospital NHS Trust
Royal Orthopaedic Hospital NHS Trust (The)
Royal Surrey County Hospital NHS Trust
Royal United Hospital Bath NHS Trust
Royal West Sussex NHS Trust
Royal Wolverhampton Hospitals NHS Trust (The)
Salford Royal Hospitals NHS Trust
Salisbury Foundation NHS Trust
Sandwell and West Birmingham Hospitals NHS Trust
Scarborough and North East Yorkshire Health Care
NHS Trust
Selby and York Primary Care Trust
Sheffield Children's NHS Trust
Sheffield Teaching Hospitals NHS Foundation Trust
Shrewsbury and Telford Hospitals NHS Trust
Shropshire County Primary Care Trust
South and East Dorset Primary Care Trust
South Birmingham Primary Care Trust
South Devon Healthcare NHS Trust
South Hams and West Devon Primary Care Trust
South Manchester University Hospitals NHS Trust
South Somerset Primary Care Trust
South Tees Hospitals NHS Trust
South Tyneside Healthcare Trust
South Warwickshire General Hospitals NHS Trust
South West Dorset Primary Care Trust
Southampton University Hospitals NHS Trust
Southend Hospital NHS Trust
Southport and Ormskirk Hospitals NHS Trust
St Albans and Harpenden Primary Care Trust
St Anthony's Hospital
St George's Healthcare NHS Trust
St Helens and Knowsley Hospitals NHS Trust
St Mary's NHS Trust
Staffordshire Moorlands Primary Care Trust
Stockport NHS Foundation Trust
Suffolk West Primary Care Trust
Surrey & Sussex Healthcare NHS Trust
Sussex Downs and Weald Primary Care Trust

Swansea NHS Trust
Swindon & Marlborough NHS Trust
Tameside and Glossop Acute Services NHS Trust
Taunton & Somerset NHS Trust
Tendring Primary Care Trust
Torbay Primary Care Trust
Tower Hamlets Primary Care Trust
Trafford Healthcare NHS Trust
Trafford North Primary Care Trust
Ulster Community & Hospitals NHS Trust
United Bristol Healthcare NHS Trust
United Lincolnshire Hospitals NHS Trust
University College London Hospitals NHS
Foundation Trust
University Hospital Birmingham NHS Foundation Trust
University Hospital of North Staffordshire NHS Trust
University Hospitals Coventry and Warwickshire
NHS Trust
University Hospitals of Leicester NHS Trust
Uttlesford Primary Care Trust
Vale of Aylesbury Primary Care
Walsall Hospitals NHS Trust
West Dorset General Hospitals NHS Trust
West Gloucestershire Primary Care Trust
West Hertfordshire Hospitals NHS Trust
West Middlesex University Hospital NHS Trust
West Suffolk Hospitals NHS Trust
West Wiltshire Primary Care Trust
Weston Area Health Trust
Whipps Cross University Hospital NHS Trust
Whittington Hospital NHS Trust
Winchester & Eastleigh Healthcare NHS Trust
Wirral Hospital NHS Trust
Worcestershire Acute Hospitals
Worthing and Southlands Hospitals NHS Trust
Wrightington, Wigan & Leigh NHS Trust
Wycombe Primary Care Trust
York Hospitals NHS Trust
Yorkshire Wolds & Coast Primary Care Trust

Specialist centres

Beckenham Hospital (Sickle Cell Site)
Homerton Hospital (Care Antenatal Clinic)
Keighley Health Centre
Kings College Hospital (Sickle Cell Site)
Royal London Hospital (Department of Haematology)
Sickle Cell & Thalassaemia Department (Bradford)
Sickle Cell & Thalassaemia Centre (Brent)
Sickle Cell & Thalassaemia Centre (Bristol)
Sickle & Thalassaemia Centre (Cardiff)
Sickle Cell & Thalassaemia Centre (City & Hackney)
Sickle Cell & Thalassaemia Centre (City Hospital)
Sickle & Thalassamia Service (Coventry)
Sickle Cell & Thalassaemia Service (Croydon)
Sickle & Thalassaemia Centre (Gloucester)
Sickle Cell & Thalassaemia Service (Hammersmith & Fulham)
Sickle Cell & Thalassaemia Centre (Hounslow)
Sickle Cell & Thalassaemia Centre (Ladywood Heath Centre)
Sickle & Thalassaemia Centre (Leeds)
Sickle Cell & Thalassaemia Centre (Leicester)
Sickle & Thalassaemia Service (Luton)
Sickle & Thalassaemia Service (Milton Keynes)
Sickle & Thalassaemia Centre (Newham)
Sickle Cell & Thalassaemia Service (Nottingham)
Sickle & Thalassaemia Service (Reading)
Sickle & Thalssaemia Centre (Sandwell)
Sickle Cell & Thalassaemia Service (Sheffield)
Sickle Cell & Thalassaemia Service (Southampton)
Sickle & Thalassaemia Centre (South West London)
Department of Haematology (St Thomas' Hospital)
Sickle Cell & Thalassaemia Service (Walsall)
Sickle Cell & Thalassaemia Support Project (Wolverhampton)

Appendix C

Governance of NCEPOD

The National Confidential Enquiry into Patient Outcome and Death (NCEPOD) is an independent body to which a corporate commitment has been made by the Medical and Surgical Colleges, Associations and Faculties related to its area of activity. Each of these bodies nominates members on to NCEPOD's Steering Group.

Steering Group as at 21st November 2007

Dr D Whitaker	Association of Anaesthetists of Great Britain and Ireland
Mr T Bates	Association of Surgeons of Great Britain & Ireland
Mr J Wardrope	College of Emergency Medicine
Dr S Bridgman	Faculty of Public Health Medicine
Dr P Cartwright	Royal College of Anaesthetists
Dr P Nightingale	Royal College of Anaesthetists
Dr B Ellis	Royal College of General Practitioners
Ms M McElligott	Royal College of Nursing
Prof D Luesley	Royal College of Obstetricians and Gynaecologists
Mrs M Wishart	Royal College of Nursing
Dr I Doughty	Royal College of Paediatrics and Child Health
Dr R Dowdle	Royal College of Physicians
Professor T Hendra	Royal College of Physicians
Dr M Armitage	Royal College of Physicians
Dr M Clements	Royal College of Physicians
Dr A Nicholson	Royal College of Radiologists
Mr B Rees	Royal College of Surgeons of England
Mr M Parker	Royal College of Surgeons of England
Mr D Mitchell	Faculty of Dental Surgery, Royal College of Surgeons of England
Dr S Lishman	Royal College of Pathologists
Ms S Panizzo	Patient Representative
Mrs M Wang	Patient Representative

Observers

Mrs C Miles	Institute of Healthcare Management
Dr R Palmer	Coroners' Society of England and Wales
Mrs H Burton	Scottish Audit of Surgical Mortality
Mrs E Stevenson	National Patient Safety Agency
Dr K Cleary	National Patient Safety Agency
Professor P Littlejohns	National Institute for Health and Clinical Excellence

NCEPOD is a company, limited by guarantee and a registered charity, managed by Trutees.

Trustees

Chairman	Professor T Treasure
Treasurer	Professor G T Layer
	Professor M Britton
	Professor J H Shepherd
	Mr M A M S Leigh
	Dr D Justins
Company Secretary	Dr M Mason

Clinical Co-ordinators

The Steering Group appoint a Lead Clinical Co-ordinator for a defined tenure. In addition there are six Clinical Co-ordinators who work on each study. All Co-ordinators are engaged in active academic/clinical practice (in the NHS) during their term of office.

Lead Clinical Co-ordinator

Mr I C Martin	(Surgery)

Clinical Co-ordinators

Dr D G Mason	(Anaesthesia)
Dr J Stewart	(Medicine)
Professor S B Lucas	(Pathology)
Dr G Findlay	(Intensive Care)
Dr D Mort	(Medicine)
Mr M Lansdown	(Surgery)